The Camp Wise Story
1907-1988

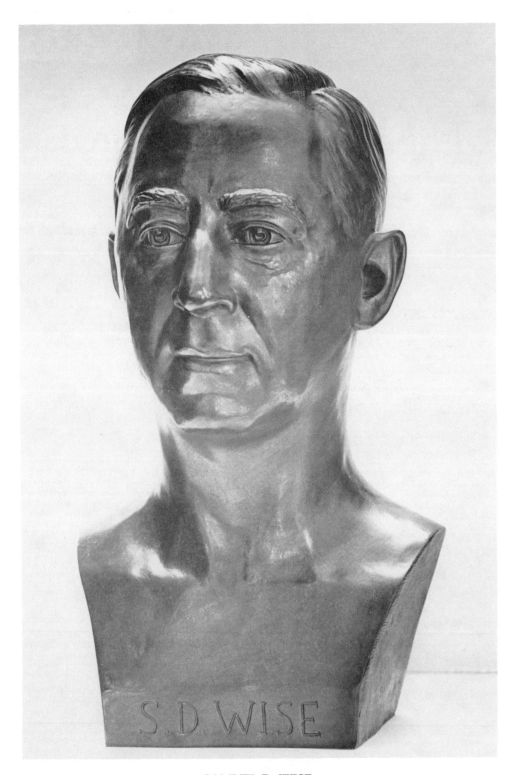

SAMUEL D. WISE
Paris, 1930
Photograph by Al Willinger, 1989

The Camp Wise Story
1907-1988

by
Albert M. Brown

Editors

David B. Guralnik   Judah Rubinstein

Cleveland, Ohio
The Jewish Community Federation
in cooperation with
The Western Reserve Historical Society

Jewish Community Federation
1750 Euclid Avenue
Cleveland, Ohio 44115-2144

Western Reserve Historical Society
10825 East Boulevard
Cleveland, Ohio 44106

To
all leaders,
past and present,
who helped bring
joy and precious memories
to thousands of children
at
Camp Wise

HELLO CAMP WISE

How-do-you-do, Camp Wise
How-do-you-do?
How-do-you-do, Camp Wise
How-do-you-do?
We're so glad to see you here,
We've been waiting for a year,
How-do-you-do, Camp Wise
How-do-you-do?

Acknowledgments

This book was made possible through the interest and support of two families who trace directly to the beginnings of Camp Wise — the first to its founder, Samuel D. Wise, and the second to an outstanding early leader and life-time trustee, William C. Treuhaft. Today, this association continues through H. Jack and Frances Wise Lang and Howard Wise for the Samuel D. Wise and May Wise Philanthropic Fund of the Jewish Community Federation and through Elizabeth M. Treuhaft for the Treumart Fund, a supporting foundation of the Federation and the Cleveland Foundation.

It is the fifth title in the publication program of the Jewish Community Federation, which is devoted to preserving in print the story of Cleveland Jewish life. It was prepared under the aegis of the Publication Subcommittee (chaired by David I. Sindell) and of the Archives and History Committee (chaired by Lloyd S. Schwenger). Most helpful were the guidance of the Endowment Fund Department and the encouragement of Stephen H. Hoffman, executive vice president of the Federation.

A special note of appreciation is extended to the Library of the Western Reserve Historical Society and its director, Kermit J. Pike, especially its reprographer, Michael McCormick, and the Society's Cleveland Jewish Archives. Mort Epstein, Epstein Gutzwiller & Partners, is most esteemed for his attractive cover and book design and for his personal interest in bringing this book to light.

Contents

Preface

In eight decades from its beginnings in 1907, Camp Wise developed from a simple fresh-air camp into a highly organized camping facility. As it moved from its first home near Euclid, Ohio (Stein-on-the-Lake, Interurban Stop 133), to Painesville in 1924, and to Halle Park in Burton in 1966 (technically the camp is located in Claridon Township), it expanded to make the world of nature a bright part of the lives of thousands of children and teenagers, initially for immigrant families, and now for the entire Cleveland Jewish community.

The history opens with the generous gift of Samuel D. Wise to the community and the dedicated pioneer efforts of Camp Wise Association leaders, among them Eugene Geismer, Rabbi Moses Gries, and Hilda Mulhauser. Still other Association members and trustees continued to build Camp Wise, leaders like William Treuhaft, Ida Schott, David Warshawsky, David Apple, Hugo Mahrer, Leon Weil, Henry Marcuson, and Arthur Dettelbach. On the staff side, the Camp began its first decades under the leadership of Abel and Alex Warshawsky, Dr. Oscar Markey, Grace Grossman, and Albert Kinoy. Its transitional years from Painesville to Burton were guided by Herman Eigen, executive director of the Jewish Community Center, and Abe Bonder, director of Camp Wise. These and many others are the leaders, volunteers, and staff, who gave direction to the Camp and whose names echo in its life today

The book also has a unique focus because Albert Brown's account of Cleveland Jewish camping is also his personal memoir in its first two decades. Camp Wise diverted him away from the business world to a fulfilling career in the Jewish Center field. For Al Brown, Camp Wise became and remains to this day the Home of Happiness.

A number of special sections enrich Al's narrative — David Warshawsky's autobiographical chapter on his teenage experiences at Camp; the 1911 diary of volunteer leaders; the pages from *Personal and Professional* by Sidney Vincent, relating his role at Camp during the depression and early wartime years; a chronicle drawn primarily from the Camp Wise Association records; some brief social notes from the Alliwise Association bulletin; and a selection of song parodies, which flavored every hike and evening campfire session. In addition, a selection of historic and contemporary photographs supplement the written pages and fuse image to word. A code letter in each photograph caption refers to the list of sources below.

The Camp Wise Story will be a valued addition to the written record of Cleveland Jewish social history. It will be cherished by all who have experienced Camp Wise or who otherwise appreciate its place in our community, yesterday and today.

Photograph Credits

A. Sabina Berman
B. Albert M. Brown
C. Cleveland Jewish Archives, Western Reserve Historical Society
D. Jewish Community Center, Cleveland
E. Jewish Community Federation of Cleveland
F. Charles Koch
G. Dr. Oscar Markey
H. Berni Rich, Score Photographers
I. Florence Warshawsky, Abel G. Warshawsky Album
J. Rose Weinberg

Albert Brown's narrative of Camp Wise moves on two paths through its more than eight decades of Cleveland Jewish camping life. The first, personal in participation and experience, covers the period 1907-1927 of his own direct association as a camper, staff leader, and director. After this first phase, he followed the progress of Camp Wise as a member of Cleveland's Council Educational Alliance staff for two years, next as a group work professional in the Bronx, New York, and Toledo for almost 25 years, and lastly, since 1955, as a professional social work executive for Cleveland organizations and in retirement. In brief then, this account is a mix of Al Brown's own memories and what he has absorbed in closely following the story of Camp Wise, which for him as a youngster, leader, and intimate observer and contributor, has always been the "Home of Happiness."

Biographical details about Albert Brown are given on the back cover of this volume. But it is "My 'Home of Happiness' " that tells you about the man and his life-long dedication to Cleveland Jewish camping and the way each enriched the other.

My "Home of Happiness"

Albert M. Brown

INTRODUCTION

Organized camping is more than 125 years old, as the first organized children's camp of which we know was set up in 1861. Settlement house camps began around the turn of the century. Among the landmarks was the founding of the Educational Alliance camp at Cold Springs, New York, in 1901, later to be sponsored by the New York 92nd Street YMHA. In the 1920's it was incorporated as the legendary Surprise Lake Camp. The Henry Street Settlement in New York and Hull House in Chicago were also among the first to start camps for children and for mothers with babies. These social agencies around the country were deeply concerned with the condition and social needs of the millions of immigrants, including the Jewish immigrants from Eastern Europe, who came to America mainly during the decades from 1880 to 1914.

By 1910, at least 75 Jewish neighborhood centers and settlement houses — as well as many settlement houses under nonsectarian auspices serving large numbers of the Jewish population — had been founded. These settlements provided the core of community leadership for the planning and building of summer camps. They were created to give underprivileged children an opportunity to leave the hot, crowded city streets for a brief holiday in the country.

These early camps were organized essentially as social welfare agencies, with philanthropic lay leaders as members of boards of trustees having responsibility for financial support, policy making, and selection of staff for the camps. Campers came from the most economically underprivileged Jewish families and paid minimal fees, if any.

Counselors were volunteers who usually served for two weeks. Because the founders of these camps wished to serve as many children as possible, camping periods were generally limited to from ten days to two weeks. Most emphasis was placed on "fresh air," clean, healthy atmosphere, and enhancing the physical well-being of undernourished children. In line with this concept — to give local Jewish children an opportunity for a brief holiday in the "fresh air" — and in this same period of the beginnings of the camp movement, Camp Wise was founded in 1907.

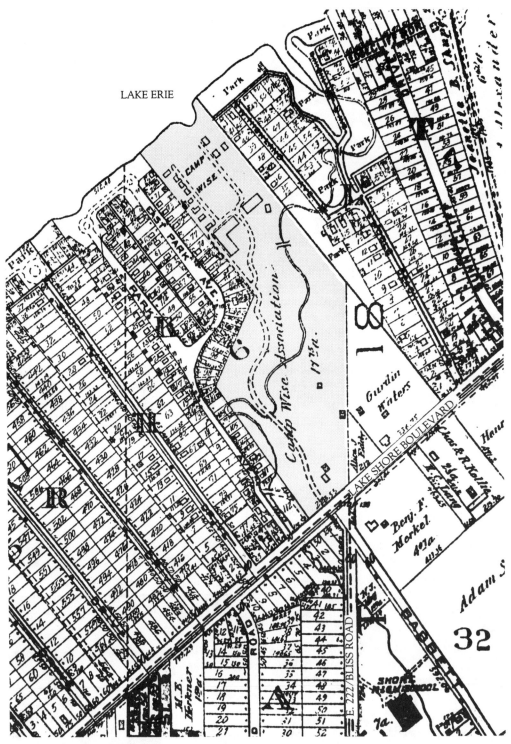

LAKE ERIE

Camp Wise, first site (1907-1923), Euclid, Ohio, Cuyahoga County.
G.M. Hopkins Plat Book, 1920. (C)
Note: The road to the east of the camp, then called Bliss Rd., is now E. 222d St.

I.
IN THE BEGINNING: STOP 133, LAKE SHORE BOULEVARD
1907 to 1923

In the spring of 1907 — more than four score years ago — the National Council of Jewish Women, Cleveland Section, in cooperation with the settlement house they had started, decided on a summer project, a camp for children. "Fresh air camps" were just beginning to flourish throughout the country. This pioneering idea came to them about ten years after the Cleveland Section — hereinafter to be designated as the Council — was first organized.

The Council came into existence in 1894 through the amalgamation of several social-philanthropic women's groups and affiliated with the national organization in 1896. In a small rented house on Orange Avenue it began classes in English, cooking, and sewing, along with clubs for boys and girls, a public bathhouse, and a day nursery. But with the ever-increasing number of immigrants coming to Cleveland, there was a need and demand for more citizenship classes and recreational programs for children, all of which required more funds, larger quarters, and more volunteers for these increased services.

Mrs. Flora Schwab, then president of the Council, with her wise leadership and social vision, brought together a group of prominent men and women of the Jewish community and suggested a settlement house on the order of the famous Hull House in Chicago, the Henry Street Settlement in New York, and Hiram House on Orange Avenue in Cleveland. Out of this meeting, addressed by Rabbi Moses Gries, plans were developed for a "gigantic" charity ball and bazaar, which quickly became the talk of the town. As a result of this enthusiasm, the Council raised the impressive amount of $11,000, which in that era was a history-making achievement. The year was 1898.

That fall a spacious home and property at 300 Woodland Avenue was donated by Moritz and Yetta Joseph to the Council. Soon after, on April 6, 1899, the settlement house, now officially named the Council Educational Alliance, was incorporated to "engage in educational, recreational and philanthropic work." These names are recorded at that first Board meeting: Flora Schwab, Bella Wiener, Molly Stearn, Barney Mahler, Edward M. Baker, Jac Einstein, Sol Reinthal, Moritz Joseph and Rabbi Moses Gries. The group elected Bella Wiener president. Parenthetically, Mrs. Wiener was the mother of Ruth Einstein, a prominent member of the Council for over 50 years and a principal founder of Council Gardens, a housing complex for older adults, which opened in 1963.

On March 29, 1900, the building was officially dedicated, and one of the highlights of the ceremony was a performance by the talented Glee Club Chorus of the Girls Friendly Club under the direction of a young teacher, Ida Schott, who for many years was to play such an important role in the Camp Wise story as registrar, leader, and advisor. That year the Board also appointed Isaac Spectorsky of Denver as the first director (or head worker, as he was called then) of the Council Educational Alliance at the notable salary of $1,200 per year.

The rapid expansion of the Woodland immigrant community was to lead directly to the establishment of Camp Wise. The flood of Old Country arrivals pushed the area's Jewish population from 30,000 at the turn of the century to 60,000 by 1912. The pressure for space and housing in turn caused older area residents and their institutions, among them the Excelsior Club, the elite German-Jewish social club, to move eastward. Located at E. 37th Street and Woodland Avenue since 1887, directly in the main path of immigrant movement, the club was ready to move, as it did in 1909 to become a close neighbor of Western Reserve University. (Its building is now the Case Western Reserve University Student Union.) Negotiations were started with the Excelsior Club, through its president, Maurice Rohrheimer, for the purchase of the club property. A fund of $10,000 was raised to help buy and remodel the club. The new Council Educational Alliance was dedicated in 1909, with the Honorable Judson Harmon, Governor of Ohio, as the principal speaker. A new era had begun in the Cleveland Jewish community. Camp Wise was to be an important part of it.

After seven years of devoted and fruitful work, Isaac Spectorsky had left the Alliance, having been succeeded by Henry Wolf, with Helen Bauldauf as associate head worker. It was Miss Baldauf who, in 1907, suggested the idea of a summer camp for both children and mothers. She had visited the camp of the Henry Street Settlement and was so impressed that she urged the Board to open such a "fresh air camp in the country" for the Jewish children of Cleveland. Although not yet highly organized in philosophy and programming, these summer camps, especially for the children living in the crowded sections of New York and Pennsylvania, began to be a necessary part of settlement house activity. But until the early 20's, when the American Camping Association was officially organized, there were no accepted standards and definite policies for the summer camps in the various states. It was about this time that Charles W. Eliot, former president of Harvard, made the statement that "the summer camp is a momentous innovation, perhaps America's greatest contribution to education." The American Camping Association conducted institutes and conferences for directors in order to intensify knowledge of camping.

Early in 1907 Eugene Geismer was appointed a committee of one to call upon Samuel D. Wise, a public-spirited businessman and philanthropist, to see if he would be willing to allow the use of his summer place at Interurban Stop 133 at East 222nd Street (then Bliss Road) and Lake Shore Boulevard as a camp for children. Mr. Wise graciously consented. Hilda Muhlhauser, a staff member of the Alliance, spent that first summer as camp director, assisted by enthusiastic young men and women from Cleveland's Jewish upper society. To volunteer at Camp Wise was the "in thing" and there were many young adults who were eager to serve. The "camp experiment", as Sam Wise called it, proved to be a great success, and a permanent institution would give a much needed period of recreation and rest to children and to mothers with babies in the years ahead.

The establishment of Camp Wise quickly followed. On October 9, 1907, Rabbi Moses Gries, Isadore Grossman, Meyer Weil, and Eugene Geismer legally incorporated the Camp Wise Association. Then, five weeks later on November

18th, Sam Wise wrote them, "I will convey to your organization without reservation other than that providing for the permanent occupation of the premises for a Fresh Air Camp, the real estate including buildings, improvements, etc., of every character whatsoever, of which I am now the present owner, situated at a Noble Postoffice, Cuyahoga County, on Lake Erie and formerly known as Stein's on the Lake."

The Board happily accepted the gift. In addition to the property, Mr. Wise donated $500, Council Educational Alliance gave $1,000, the Cleveland Section $1,000, and the Federation of Jewish Charities (now the Jewish Community Federation) $1,000 toward the following year's expenses. Thus, Camp Wise, named in honor of its donor, and the Camp Wise Association, as an independent organization, came into existence.

The name Warshawsky played a prominent role at Camp Wise in those early years. David, the youngest of three brothers, spent the very first camp summer as an all-around helper in the kitchen and wherever needed. When the season was over, he suggested to Miss Muhlhauser that his older brother Abel ("Buck") would be a good leader for the next camping season in 1908, since he had had experience as playground supervisor at the Henry Street Settlement House in New York while attending art classes.

Buck Warshawsky was appointed head boys' leader of the camp for 1908 at $50 a month. He was an outgoing, handsome, athletic man, a baseball player, a pitcher, in fact, who was good enough to support himself by playing on weekends with a semi-pro team. He was the first of a succession of camp directors who were role models for the boys in camp. After the 1908 season, Buck left for Paris to continue his studies in painting. The third brother, Alex, took over the program as leader in the years 1909-10-11. In later years, both Buck and Alex became gifted artists who achieved international success. A painting by Buck Warshawsky after the 1908 season, titled "A Group of Boys Swimming at Camp Wise," was later exhibited at the Autumn Salon in Paris.

What did Camp Wise mean to a youngster in 1910? I can relate to that year in a personal way. Being a native Clevelander, born at the turn of the century of immigrant parents who had fled from pogroms in Russia, I was eligible and chosen as one of the fortunate children to attend camp for two weeks. Being sent out to the country to a place called Camp Wise was the most exciting adventure of my young life. It was my first time away from home and I hardly knew what to expect. My parents admonished me to "behave and do whatever the leaders tell you to do."

I remember that many boys and girls gathered at the Public Square, where the Old Post Office building still stands. There we waited impatiently for the welcome sound of the interurban train. With screams and shouts of joy as the train approached, mixed with tears and frantic hugs from parents, we eagerly boarded the train to be transported, as if by magic, from the turmoil of the city and hot streets into a new world of trees, green fields, fresh air, the smell of the woods and pines, and, perhaps best of all, swimming in the cool *clean* waters of

Lake Erie! But even before the train left, some children were crying because they were already homesick.

The leaders accompanying the children on the train were kind and considerate, seeing to it that we were comfortable and happy. We looked up to them with great respect and affection. I recall how my brothers and sisters talked of the wonderful men and women — "leaders" they called them — at the Council Educational Alliance, who were so helpful and friendly in their clubs, with games, stories, songs, arts and crafts, and parties. The names of Miss Schott, Miss Muhlhauser, Mr. Spectorsky, and others became household words. Now here I was, face to face, in their midst and under their care and supervision. I felt so safe!

The two weeks went by like a dream — so fast and so full of new, happy experiences. But it was my second trip to Camp Wise in 1914 that left the greatest impression upon me. It was my bar mitzvah year, and when my parents asked what I would like for a special gift, I immediately answered, "Send me to Camp Wise again!"

Like all the other campers and leaders that year, I fell under the spell of the tall, handsome, athletic-looking head leader, William Treuhaft. (In later years I was told that Bill Treuhaft was the first "professional" director of Camp Wise.)

Since I was considered one of the older campers — at age 13 — he gave me certain responsibilities over the younger children. One day he called me a "junior leader." *That* meant more to me than anything else that summer, although I still cherish the memories of the good food, the hikes, the softball games, the songs, and especially the campfires and the leaders. I was sold on camping from that day on. It became more than just a vacation in the country; it was an important and necessary part of my life. To spend a whole summer as a head leader at Camp Wise would be just about the most wonderful thing that could ever happen to me. (Ten years later, in 1924, that did happen.)

The daily schedule during those early years (1907 to 1923) did not vary except for the occasional all-day picnic hike or overnight hike. Otherwise, a day at camp followed a more or less fixed routine:

    6:30 - Rising (to Charley's bugle or a bell)
    7:00 - Exercises on the lawn before breakfast
    7:30 - Breakfast - clean-up squads - room inspection
    9:30 - Assembly - songs - announcements of activities: group programs - hikes - sports - games - arts and crafts - dramatics - stories
  11:00 - General swim and swimming lessons
  12:15 - Lunch
    1:00 - Rest hour (leader in charge)
    2:15 - Another assembly - afternoon activities
    4:00 - Swimming and swimming lessons
    5:00 - Free hour
    6:00 - Dinner - followed by evening program, often prepared on very short notice: outdoor lawn games, sports, and almost nightly, the campfire, with everyone gathering around to sing songs and tell

stories. Sometimes marshmallows were toasted, or some generous person would donate watermelon. Once each trip, after the evening meal, the campers would enjoy watching the leaders-campers softball game, rooting for their favorites

Eventually the recreation room and large play area made more varied evening programs possible:

Monday	Campfire
Tuesday	Moving picture show (*silent* movies!) brought out from town by the UBY's [part-time volunteer leaders who came out to camp evenings and weekends]
Wednesday	Dance
Thursday	Campers' stunt night
Friday	Stories and, beginning in 1918, biblical plays
Saturday	Circus, once each trip, or minstrel show, and, beginning in 1918, Sabbath services
Sunday	Masquerade and dance
Special Events:	Track meet, treasure hunt, hare and hound chase, college day, Indian lore, international group stunts, charades, shadowgraphs

Many special events and happenings mark the early decades at Stop 133. In chronological order, here are some of the highlights:

1907   When Samuel D. Wise gave his consent to allow the use of his property on Lake Shore for a summer camp, the first group consisted of 25 boys from Council Educational Alliance and 25 girls selected by the National Council of Jewish Women, Cleveland Section. They stayed for two weeks and were followed by the same number for another two weeks —a total of 100 boys and girls that first summer.

Hilda Muhlhauser had charge of the camp, assisted by a volunteer, Delo Mook, who was supervisor of the boys.

This vacation in the country for 100 children was heralded in the Jewish community of Cleveland as a wonderful innovation.

1908   This was really the first year that the camp was called Camp Wise, since it was in the fall of 1907 that the Camp Wise Association was legally formed to conduct the affairs of the camp. A grant of $2,400 from the Federation of Jewish Charities was given to Camp Wise with the provision that at least 100 persons would be at camp each summer. The Association also passed a motion that $5,000 be raised by contributions from the Jewish community.

Thus, Camp Wise was already becoming an important and integral agency in the Jewish community.

This year, 1908, in addition to Abel Warshawsky, head leader, Charley Dietz was employed as year-round caretaker at $12 per week. The Board voted the next year to buy a horse for this popular caretaker at a cost of $50. Charley would now be able to follow the campers on their all-day picnic hike to the Nine-Mile Creek and bring the food by horse and wagon. A gardener, cook's assistant, athletic coach, and one-man music band, Charley Dietz was truly a master handy man. He was also the bugle-blower for early morning wake-up, and with this duty he was not always so popular.

1909   Alex Warshawsky was hired in his brother Abel's place as head leader. After the first two weeks of this season, mothers with babies were accepted as campers. Campers fees: 50 cents to $1.00.

1910   Samuel Wise arranged for the installation of electric lights in camp. An emergency "hospital" was set up to take care of the campers, if and when needed. A cottage for mothers with babies was erected, donated by Mrs. J. B. Stotter.

This was also the year that a group of young men who worked in town came out to camp every night after work and every weekend as volunteer leaders. They were allowed to pitch a tent on the grounds and in later years they were given permission to build a cabin. They were extremely helpful in many ways. The group gave themselves the name of the UBY's, which was supposed to be a secret name. Actually the name is merely ABC language for "You Be Wise."

They remained loyal volunteers through the first three decades, among them Leon Weil, Henry Marcuson, Eli Drucker, Dave Sheinbart, Moe Gimp, Dick Shoenberger, Saul Drucker, and Dave Warshawsky.

1911   A new sanitary system was installed. Dr. Isadore Grossman became the first camp physician.

1913   Iron steps leading down to the beach were constructed. Eugene Geismer was appointed a representative of Camp Wise to the Federation of Jewish Charities.

1914   This year an amendment to the Association constitution reads: "A leaders social committee shall arrange for leaders and workers, to provide entertainment and have general direction of the social work to be done at camp."

From this amendment came the organization to be known as the Camp Wise Crew, which, according to their constitution, was "to provide and train prospective leaders; to guide and foster the growth and development of Camp Wise; to promote the welfare and good fellowship of its members."

Dr. J. Grossman was elected the first president of the Camp Wise Crew.

1916   Lillian Bauman was elected president of the Camp Wise Association.

Senior members of the Alliance were given permission to use camp for a weekend after regular season closed.

1917   Ida Schott, who had given up teaching to become a staff member of the Council Educational Alliance in 1913, was appointed social worker and registrar for Camp Wise, bringing the camp in closer contact with the Alliance. She reported total applications of *2,475 individuals* for Camp Wise; *total at camp was 778.* She also reported that the fees received from all campers and adults amounted to over $1,000, the largest total ever.

In this war year, Miss Schott took charge of camp.

The 10th Anniversary of Camp Wise was observed August 28th. Leaders and campers participated in a play, "The Laughing Cry of Peace," written by Joseph Grossman and Joseph Klein.

This year, too, marked the first indication that Jewish content should be more apparent at camp. Rabbi Louis Wolsey suggested that religious and moral education be introduced at Camp Wise.

1918   As if in reponse to Rabbi Wolsey's suggestion, Ferd Isserman, a student at Hebrew Union College, was appointed head leader for the summer. Biblical plays on Friday nights and services on Saturday mornings became regular programs.

After two summers in which senior members of the Alliance used the camp for Labor Day weekends, it was in this year that the organization that came to be known as Alliwise was given permission to have its own full week at camp following the close of the season. Walter Leo Solomon and Ida Schott, creators of the Alliwise idea, thanked the Board of Trustees of the Camp Wise Association for the use of the camp. It was a fine cooperative arrangement for many years, from 1918 into the late 50's. A full story of Alliwise is reported in a later chapter.

1919   Oscar B. Markey, a student at the University of Pittsburgh, was appointed head leader of boys at Camp Wise, and a new era began. He became camp director for the seasons of 1920 and 1921. Mainly because of his charisma and leadership the Camp Wise Crew became a more active and integral part of camp. Mr.

Markey brought new ideas in programs and songs to camp, and campers and leaders responded to make the camp trips more enjoyable than ever before.

The Federation of Jewish Charities donated the sum of $8,000 for this camp season.

Officers of the Camp Wise Association were: William Treuhaft, President; Dr. J. Grossman, Vice-president; Tina Bernstein, Secretary; and Samuel D. Wise, Treasurer.

1921   At the Board meeting of the Association, there was a special vote of thanks and commendation to Oscar Markey, who was going on to medical school, for his three years of service to the camp. Dr. Markey, who later married a staff member, Claire Feldman, made his home in Cleveland and continued his interest in Camp Wise for many years as board member and president of the Association.

At this same meeting of the Board, announcement was made that Miss Grace Grossman would be director in 1922 and 1923 and hopefully the first director in 1924 of the "new" camp in Painesville

1922   Harry Weinberg was head leader of boys and Louise Affelder, girls' leader for the 1922-23 seasons, under the supervision of the director.

At this time it was decided to place the Camp Wise property on the market. Euclid Village offered to purchase the grounds for $95,000. This money was to be used for the purchase of a new site [Painesville].

As a volunteer leader in 1921-22-23, I learned anew how eagerly the youngsters looked forward to free outdoor life, with exciting experiences — swimming, games, sports, trips, campfires, making friends, happy events, and pleasant memories.

But camp means different things to people individually. Many parents probably regard camp with mixed emotions. They may feel the wrench of separation from their children; they may enjoy — sometimes with slight guilt feelings — the leisure and shift of responsibility that result from handing over the care of their children to camp leaders and directors.

They hope that after the summer's experience their children will come home in better health and with happier dispositions and that they will have developed desirable and enjoyable skills in games and sports and perhaps learned more of nature and music.

This is what *some* parents hope for their children. Others will be satisfied just to have them home again, safe and sound and healthy! But it seemed to me in those early years that to the children who came to Camp Wise, camp meant just one thing — FUN! Leaders were expected to see to it that the campers in their care were enjoying themselves to the fullest. That seemed to be the main purpose of camp. But gradually, even in the 20's, there came the realization among camp professionals that while having fun was worthwhile, there were also other important factors.

Staff members with special training in arts and crafts, dramatics, nature study, dance, and music were hired when the new Camp Wise opened in 1924.

The volunteer leaders may not have had the expertise in camping that the trained staff had, but they did possess priceless qualifications: youth, enthusiasm, some specialized skills, a willingness to please, and, above all, a sincere, natural liking for children. Volunteerism during these years was something beautiful to behold at Camp Wise.

On the recommendation of Ida Schott, I reported to Oscar Markey, director, in August, 1921, to serve as a volunteer leader for a two-week trip. Just as Buck Warshawsky, his brother Alex, and Bill Treuhaft were idolized, so did campers, as well as leaders, regard Oscar Markey with great devotion and respect. Due to his leadership, the two weeks were full of joy and delightful days and nights. Children actually cried when the trip was over and they had to say goodbye to Mr. Markey and the leaders. One older girl said she could now understand how Cinderella must have felt when, after the beautiful masquerade ball had ended at midnight, she had to return to her drab existence.

I shall always remember with great fondness the patience, kindness, and consideration shown to me, a neophyte counselor, by such veteran leaders as Natalie Biederman, Art Dettelbach, Eli and Saul Drucker, Claire Feldman, Irene Galoin, Moe Gimp, Henry Marcuson, Florence Printz, Dave Sheinbart, Dave Warshawsky, Leon Weil, Rhoda Wolfe,and, of course, Oscar Markey.

I could say with all honesty and sincerity that the summer of 1921 changed the course of my life. At the start of that prosperous year, I was a promising young business executive with Hiram Rivitz, president of Rivitz Plumbing Company. By the end of the year, for reasons difficult to explain, I had decided to leave and go to college to pursue a career in social work, which would include summers in the camping field. Mr. Rivitz tried to discourage me from making that decision, telling me that he had been considerering advancing me to a high position eventually. Ironically, he built the Industrial Rayon factory across the road from Camp Wise in Painesville in the late 30's, a move which at the time caused much controversy in the Jewish community.

The physical structure of Camp Wise at Stop 133, Lake Shore Boulevard, had not changed much by 1921 from the time, seven years previous, when I last came as a camper. There was the same two-story main building, which was used as the dining room and also as the "auditorium" and recreation hall for dancing, entertainments, and indoor activity on rainy days and nights.

The second floor housed the boys' sleeping quarters in small rooms — three or four in a room. The director's room was on the same floor at the head of the stairs. The girls' cottages and mothers' cottage were on one side of the field; the men leaders' cottage was on the other side. The girls' leaders slept in the girls' cottages.

The spacious grounds in front of the main hall and between the cottages were used for softball games, volleyball, races, and the inevitable daily morning exercises. At the far end of the field — quite a walk — there were those iron steps leading down to the beach and Lake Erie. On hot days the walk back from the beach was sufficient to dry the bathing suits and bodies of the swimmers. The two swim periods, morning and afternoon, were the big features of the day for the campers, if not for the leaders. They *had* to be there for supervision, whether they liked it or not. Whenever a sudden storm came up and waves were unusually high, most campers frolicked in the lake with great delight, while the leaders frantically screamed at them to come in and sometimes had to actually pull them out of the water. It is to their credit that there *never* was a swimming accident, although there were some dangerous, frightening incidents on the shores of Lake Erie. Many lives were "saved" when the lake undertow almost caused a panic. On most days, however, the swimming sessions were very enjoyable.

In 1922, a daily camp log was kept by the leaders, which reveals some interesting and humorous incidents during those summer days. Here are a few excerpts from that diary, written over sixty years ago:

> Wednesday noon, during lunch, we sang farewell songs to Mr. Markey on his last day as director of Camp Wise. He had to leave for Pittsburg where he was to serve his year's hospital residency and internship. The children nearly broke the chairs and dishes when he started to leave. His car could hardly drive down the road through the mob of crying and shouting children. It was a sight none of us will ever forget. In writing of events in this log, it is difficult to think of words to express the feelings and emotions of that moment.

> We hiked to the nine-mile creek and were caught in a terrific storm but not before we ate our sandwiches. We practically swam back to camp! Those awaiting us welcomed us with the news that they had been holding down our tents all afternoon. The recreation hall served as Noah's Ark where we played games and songs and told stories.
>
> Dave W. told a story about India rubber and stretched it out for 20 minutes! When the storm abated somewhat and after rowing the kids to bed we retired to the recreation hall and collapsed!

> Friday was the big game of the week — the Leaders against the

campers. Heinie Marcuson came out for the weekend and brought a 15 year old boy with him as a guest for the weekend. The big kid played on the side of the leaders and won the game with a home run. The campers filed a protest because they said that the boy, called "Shondor" [Birns], was not a leader and should not have been allowed to play.

The week opened as we welcomed the most grown-up and sophisticated-looking batch of kids we have had in many years. . . . It was really heart-rending to see the poor condition of some children. For example, two of them came out in their own car with a chauffeur! We thought they wanted to buy the place and we immediately ushered them into the only room with a bath. . . . After supper, the whole camp joined in outdoor games and then a glorious bonfire. The flames reflected a circle of laughing faces as leaders and children put on an impromptu but enjoyable entertainment. As we sang "Goodnight, Ladies," it brought a happy close to a full and happy day at camp.

This is the year that William C. Treuhaft, once director of the camp himself, is now the president of the Camp Wise Association. What a guy! When he comes out to camp to visit, he acts just like one of the fellows and not like a president at all! That's why he is so well-liked. And another swell person, Leo Neumark is president of the Camp Wise Crew this year.

There is a boy in camp who pronounces his r's like w's. During rest hour one day this week, when all campers are supposed to rest on their beds, a leader discovered the boy reading a book in a corner of the room instead of resting on his bed. When told he must *rest* and not *read*, he answered: "I didn't come here to *west* — I came here to *wead*."

One of the campers said: "What are we going to have tonight in the *operation* hall?" He must have seen some of the leaders *cut up* in the *recreation* hall last night. Ouch!

Grace Grossman called a special meeting of the leaders and gave us hell for overdoing it at night by staying up much too late. She tried being a good sport by staying up with us one night because we were having such a good time singing and telling stories on the cliff and she thought that was an exception because we were relaxing after a strenuous day. But when we took advantage and stayed out late "cliffing" — some under blankets — she laid the law down and gave it to us good and heavy. She's such a wonderful person, we felt kind of ashamed and promised not to do it again. . .

———

Harry Weinberg, our head leader, informed the ladies of the Crew that he is making appointments for reading "bumps." Several ladies bumped into each other pretty hard in the rush to sign up.

———

The minstrel show was a big hit. We finally heard the joke that is the favorite one for Leon Weil. Interlocutor asks him: "Why does a jackass prefer thistles to corn?" Leon Weil answers: "That's easy. Because he's a jackass."

Because we feel that this has been an important trip in the annals of Camp Wise, we want to record the following for posterity! Week of June 19 to 26, 1922: The good ship Camp Wise started upon its 16th voyage with the indomitable Grace Grossman at the helm.

Members of the leaders crew were:

Grace Grossman	Harry Weinberg
Louise Affelder	Dr. Fetterman
Florence Printz	Milton Grossman
Claire Feldman	Sidney Galvin
Mildred Wertheim	Art Dettelbach
Edith Gross	Wilbur Steuer
Mabel Sampliner	Henry Hertz
Cyril Galvin	Mickey Weitz

Weekend Leaders

Dave Warshawsky	Moe Gimp
Leon Weil	Dave Sheinbart
Henry Marcuson	Al Brown

———

During the winter of 1921, a "Manual for Leaders" was written by members of the Camp Wise Crew. These two paragraphs reveal the spirit of Camp Wise.

The mornings at camp . . . after breakfast each child has his special work, which occupies him for only a short time, work such as sweeping their rooms, cleaning the campus and other small tasks. The children enjoy these squad duties because the leaders' association with them adds a glamour to the peeling of potatoes or sweeping the floors. "It is the joining in of the leaders with the children in work as well as play that makes Camp Wise the successful camp that it is . . . ."

The mothers must not be forgotten in our day. They do enjoy camp and are so easily satisfied and entertained; in fact they just take pleasure in watching their children and their friends' children romp and play and thrive in the good, fresh air. They also do not mind assisting whenever and wherever they can, either in the kitchen and keeping their cottage clean, even washing windows on Fridays to keep the Sabbath clean and holy. . . . This is the true spirit of Camp Wise!

By the early 20's, it became apparent that Camp Wise in Euclid was no longer considered "out in the country." Houses were being built nearby and the postwar years brought population and business enterprises too close to the camp. A new site was needed. That site was found in 1922 in a beautiful area in Painesville, Ohio, about 30 miles from Public Square.

The Board of Trustees approved the purchase of the Storrs and Harrison property in Painesville for $75,000. In preparation for moving to the new location, the Board hired George Jackson, a farmer and expert mechanic, to be the resident caretaker. It proved to be a master stroke and a most important appointment, as will be revealed in later chapters. A gift of $10,000 from Samuel D. Wise for the new camp was announced, and Charles C. Colman, architect, began to prepare plans and sketches.

After 17 years at Interurban Stop 133, Lake Shore Boulevard, Camp Wise was to close. The leaders for the final two weeks of that last 1923 season were aware that Camp Wise history was being made. While we felt sentimental about saying goodbye to the camp, there was also a kind of giddy desire to have some fun that last evening. After many suggestions, we hit upon an idea and made plans to go through with it.

One of the most popular individuals among counselors, staff, and campers was Sally Blondes, the camp nurse. She was not only an efficient and kindly person but a very good "sport" on many occasions. We also knew her to be a very sound sleeper. She slept alone in a small fabricated, plywood cabin with a removable roof. During the day, we unscrewed the roof so that it could be easily lifted at night while she slept. Sometime after midnight, on what we believed would be a clear night, we did lift the roof, leaving the nurse sound asleep, with the sky overhead.

Back in the recreation hall, like mischievous children, we laughed and joked about it when suddenly we heard raindrops falling on the roof of the building! The joke had gone far enough. We dashed out to rescue our "wet nurse" and we carried the bed, with her on it, of course, into the recreation hall. Then we dashed out again to put the roof back on the cabin, changed her wet blanket for a dry one, carried her bed — with her on it — back into the cabin. She slept soundly through it all. However, when she awoke the next morning she told us she had had the strangest dream. While she could not recall every detail, she said it had something to do with being carried to a boat, having a good time, and then the rains came!

Old Camp Wise closed for good on Sunday, August 31st. Along with the other volunteer leaders, I was there the last two weeks and observed the event. The *Jewish Independent* headlined the end of a Cleveland camping era: "BID FAREWELL TO PRESENT CAMP WISE — LAST CAMP WISE CELEBRATION AT STOP 133." But the news story in the last paragraph noted that the curtain on the second camp was already going up. "Camp Wise will soon be closed — for all time at Stop 133 — but the Camp Wise Crew plan activities during the fall and winter to keep all in readiness for the opening of the new camp next summer."

II.
THE SECOND SITE:
PAINESVILLE, OHIO
1924 TO 1965

Months before the opening of the new Camp Wise in Painesville, Cleveland newspapers printed feature stories about the camp that "promises to be the model camp of the entire country." Models of the camp, made by the architect, Charles C. Colman, attracted considerable attention when they were displayed during Community Fund Week in the window of the J.M. Gasser Company, florists on Euclid Avenue. One of the newspaper stories included this sentence: "Camp Wise, formerly located at Stop 133, Lake Shore Boulevard, has been the 'Home of Happiness' for thousands of children and adults during its seventeen years of existence."

Excerpts from the Cleveland *Plain Dealer* described the new camp:

Built in the style of the Southern Colonial with wide siding painted white, the buildings will be grouped in formal arrangement and will be landscaped to blend the entire scheme with encircling woods. . .

There will be eight buildings with provisions made in the layout for the addition of others. . . . . The central building, with an inviting two-story portico of the type of Mt. Vernon, will contain the large recreation hall with its ample stage and dressing room facilities. . . . Flanking wings will take care of the administration offices and girl leaders' dormitories on one side and the library writing room and boy leaders' dormitories on the other side. . . . To the rear and joined to the recreation hall by a covered colonnade — with a formal garden between — will be the large dining hall, with ample kitchen facilities. . . . The children will be housed in cottages, each with its own sitting and play room and fireplace. . . . Mothers and infants will be quartered in similar buildings, with a separate room for each mother, nurses quarters, diet kitchen, laundry and large screened play porches.

Charles Colman made his architect's report to the Board of Trustees of the Camp Wise Association in 1924, before the opening. He stated:

This Camp Wise, so different from the old camp on Lake Shore Boulevard for seventeen years, was planned on sound experiences gathered at the old camp over many years by one who was a counselor and who lived the camp as it grew in makeshift fashion and by one who thought there to be given than a mere vacation in the country. . . . The buildings are painted pure white on the

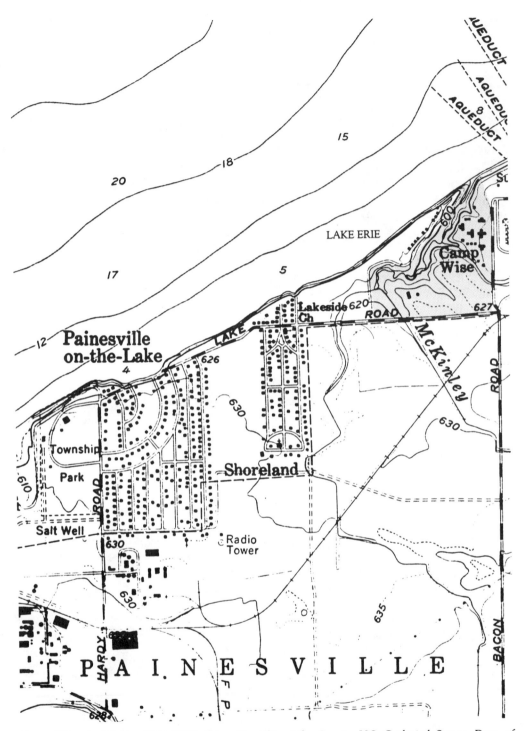

Camp Wise, second site (1924-1965), Painesville, Ohio, Lake County. U.S. Geological Survey, Dept. of Interior, 1970 rev.

exterior with the simple relief of green shutters. . . . There is the chance for an abundance of light and air in all the buildings, and every room is flooded with sunshine at some period of the day. . . . The grounds are extensive enough to provide, as was intended by the Board of Trustees, when the large acreage was purchased, recreational facilities for an increased number of institutions. Already the Jewish Orphan Home administration and the Seniors Alumni of the Council Educational Alliance, known as Alliwise, are planning to take advantage of this oportunity to partake of the facilities. . . . It is destined to be a beginning of a new era in Social Welfare in Cleveland in truly making Camp Wise the "Home of Happiness."

With the opening of the new Camp Wise in Painesville also came a change in its functions. Primarily established as a place where underprivileged Jewish boys and girls, and mothers with babies, could come for a two-week vacation, the earliest years were devoted to giving the campers a "good time." The changing program, no longer just for underprivileged children, attempted to carry on activities, such as handcraft, campcraft, nature study, and pioneer camping, all with the new concept of including Jewish content, especially in music and song and dance.

There was a television series in the 60's called "That Was The Week That Was." When I think of the first week at the new camp in Painesvile, Ohio, in 1924, the best way to describe it is to also say THAT Was The Week That Was! There will probably never be another week like that one at Camp Wise. At least, let's hope not.

In the spring of 1924, I heard the welcome news that I had been selected as boys' head leader to assist the director, Grace Grossman, for the coming camp summer. I would be completing my first year as boys' worker at the Kinsman Branch, Council Educational Alliance, and I was being given the three months away from the Alliance to accept the job at Camp Wise. I was very happy about it. I felt that it was the best job I could ever have, and I could hardly wait to get out to camp in June and get started on the ten-week camp season!

When I did arrive three days before the opening day, I could hardly believe my eyes. It seemed impossible that the camp could open within three days. Because of the unusually heavy rains for many days, the camp buildings were not yet completed. Workmen were hammering away frantically, ditch-diggers were still laying pipes along the ground, and trucks, loaded with heavy material, could hardly get through to the main road. It had been raining so steadily that the roads leading to the camp site, which were not yet paved, made it almost impossible to come within a hundred yards of it. But "come hell or high water," the first camp trip was scheduled to start on Thursday morning, June 26th, and the trip could not be postponed. The staff, under the inspired leadership of Grace Grossman, worked day and night to try to get things in shape for opening day. There was little sleep for any of us the night before. We had nothing to offer but sweat, toil, tears, and prayers!

The next morning, in raincoats and boots — yes, it was still raining — we saw the buses come down "that lonesome road" (the title of a camp song) and heard the voices of children. They were happily shouting and carrying and dragging their baggage to the recreation hall. Mothers with babies in their arms were trudging through the mud and rain. Leaders and bus drivers, and workmen too, all trying to help as best they could. It was a sight never to be forgotten and is talked about to this day by those who were there. Amazingly oblivious to the weather conditions, the children ran to the tents — temporary quarters for the campers until the cottages could be completed — with gleeful shouts, ready to start their "vacation." How could we help but love them for their innocence and enthusiasm?

After registration and assignments, it was time for lunch. Even the noise and bedlam was a welcome sound. It was organized bedlam! The orderly meals and discipline would wait until everyone could calm down. They were too excited and hungry. In fact, if this terrible pun can be excused, the excitement was *in tents*! Since there was no chance for any outdoor activities, we had to use all our ingenuity, resources, program skills, and training to cope with those rainy days indoors. We sang and sang and sang songs until we were hoarse; we played games and told stories; we improvised stunts and skits in one day that we had planned for many evening programs. But with lightning and thunder overhead, we had to keep the campers and mothers with babies busy. And happy? Well, we tried!

The evening meal was a rather quiet affair. Everyone was too exhausted to make any noise. We slept through the night as best we could and hoped for a better day tomorrow. But it was not to be. It rained off and on through the next day, too, and we were indoors again practically all day. But the worst was yet to come.

On the third day, Saturday, June 28th, Camp Wise received the tag end of a destructive tornado, a disaster that caused many deaths and millions of dollars in damages in and around Lorain, Ohio. The campers and mothers with babies were just coming into the dining room when the storm struck suddenly. Tents were blown down and gone with the wind and rain. Beds and clothing were scattered all over the fields. Windows were shattered in the cottages, roofs were partially damaged. It was frightening, but fortunately — and miraculously — there were no serious injuries. We were grateful for *that*.

The campers had to sleep in makeshift beds, if they could sleep at all that night, in the recreation hall while the storm raged. We tried to drown out the sounds of thunder and lightning with camp songs and stories. The next day we did see the sun breaking through, but the best sight was to see volunteers from town, workmen, and leaders arrive early in the morning to help us in this emergency.

A small bridge across a creek had been washed away. The bridge was necessary for campers to get to the play field and to the beach. Led by George Jackson, the workmen were able to rebuild that bridge in one day. That man

Jackson never stopped working since the storm began the night before. By nightfall Sunday evening, the campers were able to sleep in their tents and cottages. Two days later we were able to play outdoors. What a welcome treat that was for everyone.

The UBY's and other volunteer leaders came out from town to help the staff and leaders during those two weeks. We exerted special efforts to give the campers a good time for the rest of the trip. It seemed almost unfair for these campers to have spent those two camp weeks in this beautiful, but inundated, camp and call it a vacation. Yet, the strange part of it all is the fact that even to this day I come across an individual who was there and hear the comment: "That was the best, the most exciting and memorable camp trip!"

The rest of the summer, the four two-week trips, went very well indeed. The staff and volunteer leaders were extremely helpful; they were as thrilled and enthusiastic at seeing the new camp as the campers were. Going through the ten weeks of camp life with all the activities and concerns was more strenuous than I had ever dreamed it would be, but I enjoyed the opportunity of working and learning under the supervision of so fine a director as Grace Grossman.

The camp was officially dedicated during the third trip on a Sunday afternoon. The ceremonies included speeches by Samuel D. Wise, William C. Treuhaft, Grace Grossman, and the mayors of Painesville and Cleveland. Special guest speakers were Rabbi Abba Hillel Silver and Rabbi Barnett Brickner.

At the dedication, Rabbi Silver made these remarks:

> The men and women who conceived the idea of Camp Wise, those whose initial generosity made it possible, and the numerous volunteers who, as members, officers and leaders, have sustained and developed it, were prompted by true vision and social responsibility.
>
> Here we are dealing not in social delinquency but the very stuff out of which the wholesomeness and normality of life are offered. You are giving the children their right to God's out-of-doors the privilege now so sadly lacking and denied to the children of the crowded streets and cities, and you are giving them an intense training in the discipline and obligation of community and group existence.

Boys and Girls of the J.O.H. at Camp Wise

One of the best of the new features at the camp in Painesville was the arrangement with the Jewish Orphan Home (J.O.H.), then on 51st and Woodland Avenue, to send fifteen boys and fifteen girls to camp every two-week trip. They were exceptionally good campers and were so appreciative of everything that camp had to offer. It was a pleasure to get to know them. There are many stories that could be told about them. Here are a few I remember:

Every so often we read articles in the newspapers about girls who want to play baseball or football on a boys' team, especially in the Little League Division. This happened at Camp Wise in the 20's. A girl from the J.O.H. was a fine all-around athlete, and she told me she had been a regular catcher on the boys' team at the J.O.H. I thought that was interesting, but when she asked to be given a chance to be the catcher for the boys' team when they played the leaders, I knew I had a problem. After a tryout she was given that chance, much to the disgust and protests of the boys. But she played a great game and from then on she was "one of the boys."

Another story. Once each trip there was one day when campers took the place of the staff and counselors. They had to plan the programs and activities just like regular counselors. On one particular trip which I'll always remember, a boy from the J.O.H. was chosen to take my place for the day. He was chosen unanimously by the counselors because he was such a good camper and not because his name happened to be Alex Brown!

He used to tell his friends in later years that it was one of the proudest and happiest days of his life. But I feel certain that a much prouder day was the one when he graduated from Ohio State Medical School and became Dr. Alex Brown. He went on to become a highly successful and prominent psychiatrist.

A third story. The circus in Camp Wise was always the high spot of each trip. We had the usual clowns and animals but the big feature was the acrobats, even if it just meant that boys would turn somersaults. The best acrobat who ever performed in Camp Wise was Julius Ludwig, a boy from the J.O.H. Had he been serious about it, he could have become a professional acrobat and perhaps joined the "big top" of Ringling Brothers Circus. Instead he chose to become a top executive at Bobbie Brooks with Maurice Saltzman, also a boy from the J.O.H. who came to Camp Wise one summer.

A final story. This is about a boy from the J.O.H. who would rather be in a play than play baseball at Camp Wise. His name was Lou Gitlitz, and when he was twelve years old he was already a veteran performer on the stage. He loved the theatre even at that age, having taken part in children's plays at the Play House and the Alliance as well as at Camp Wise. After leaving the Home, he went to Chicago and joined a theatre group; then to New York, where he became a member of Equity, adopted the stage name Lou Gilbert, and joined the famous Group Theatre of the 30's, along with such luminaries as Elia Kazan, Clifford Odets, Marlon Brando, Lee Grant, John Garfield, and others who later were stars of stage and screen. In the 50's he was a victim of the infamous McCarthy investigations, but when that was over, he again went back to the profession he loved so much. He had an important part in the movie "Viva Zapata!", a film directed by Elia Kazan with Marlon Brando in the leading role.

Lou Gilbert's best role was that of the manager of the heavyweight champion, Jack Johnson, played by James Earl Jones in "The Great White Hope." Lou played the part on Broadway for a long run and later was given the same role in the Hollywood movie. But all during his adult life, he talked about acting in plays in "those days at Camp Wise."

In the spring of 1925, the Camp Wise Board of Trustees sent me to a five-day conference at Bear Mountain, New York, conducted by the American Camping Association. Camp experts from all parts of the country were there to teach new camping techniques, philosophies, and programs reflecting the growing interest in camps, both private and institutional. The conference was the first of its kind, and the Board expected me to take notes so that the same sort of conference or institute could be organized for leaders and staff at Camp Wise.

At the Bear Mountain Conference I was most impressed with one of the lecturers, Professor Henry Miller Busch of Columbia University, who had just written and published a text book, *Leadership in Group Work*, which was fast becoming a bible for group workers. I was delighted to get well acquainted with the author, since he enjoyed a national reputation as an expert in the camping field and in group work. I suggested that he come to Camp Wise to direct our institute just prior to the start of the 1925 season. He accepted and did direct the institute, and, incidentally, he remained in Cleveland as a professor at Western Reserve University.

The other two individuals who added greatly to our first institute were Fay Welch and Hugo Mahrer, both known experts in nature lore and woodcraft. Indian lore also became a kind of fad among camps throughout the country, and Camp Wise was no exception. At the institute, we learned Indian legends, names, and dances. Cabins and tents were given Indian names. After all, were they not the original Americans? So Indian lore became popular in the 20's and 30's in contrast to the Israeli influence from the 50's to the present day, when cabins are given Hebrew names, such as Kfar Chalutzim, Kfar Ohalim, etc. These institutes became annual affairs for many years at Camp Wise, prepared and sponsored by the Camp Wise Crew.

The Strange Summer of 1925 at Camp Wise

For the first time a rabbi was added to the staff of Camp Wise on a full-time basis in 1925. Rabbi Jacob Jaffe was not a senior student at Hebrew Union College as was Ferd Isserman in 1918. He was an experienced, elderly rabbinical scholar who accepted this summer job to bring more Jewish content into the camp programs. Friday nights and Saturday mornings Rabbi Jaffe was the head man in charge. At other times he led small groups of campers in story sessions and biblical dramatics.

That same summer, for the first and only time in Camp Wise history, a non-Jew was appointed director of the camp. William C. Treuhaft, president of the Board of the Association, while in New York City on business in the spring, was also there to interview candidates for the job of directing the camp. His selection was a physical education instructor in New York schools. James White-hill had been assistant director at a private camp and came highly recommended. I was to be his assistant, in charge of activities, as I had been Grace Grossman's assistant the previous year. Mr. Treuhaft hoped that I would be learning a great deal from Mr. Whitehill and that the experience would prepare me in future years to direct a camp. I was very pleased and looked forward to working with Mr. Whitehill.

I met him at the train from New York the day before the start of the first trip. As I offered to shake hands with him, I noticed a bandage around his right thumb and he put out his left hand to greet me. He said he had an infection and was not feeling well. On the way to camp, we had a pleasant conversation in which he asked many questions about Camp Wise. When we arrived, he asked immediately to be taken to his room — the room he and I would share for the summer. He said he would like to lie down for a few hours. The few hours stretched to a few days. He was served his meals and did not venture from the room until near the end of the first week.

The camp physician and nurse were with him at various times but could find nothing seriously wrong with him. He may have had a slight fever but otherwise seemed to be in good spirits, as he consulted with me very often about the program and activities. I had to make excuses to the campers and counselors that the director of the camp was ill.

When he finally did appear in the dining room one morning, he made a good impression on everybody. He was a splendid-looking individual and had a loud, booming voice. Since he was a teacher in New York schools, it was obvious that he was a strict disciplinarian. He told me to carry on with the program and activities and he would simply observe for the first two weeks.

When the trip was over and there was a free day before the next trip would start, we spent some time together and became better acquainted. He told me quite frankly that his camp experience was limited to private camps where about 100 boys stayed for eight weeks. He wondered how we were able to cope with five two-week trips and how much the campers could absorb of camp life in only two weeks. I tried to explain that having five two-week trips of 200 campers each trip meant that we were serving over a thousand children and mothers with babies during the summer. Even that number was only a part of the total number who needed Camp Wise for two weeks.

He said he would "observe" again for the next two weeks and would then be able to take over and direct the camp for the rest of the summer. In the meantime, the camp was operating smoothly with the kind of routine and activities that the staff had been accustomed to. There were very few suggestions or new ideas from the director. One day Rabbi Jaffe and many of the counselors wanted to know how it happened that a Catholic was appointed director at the same time that a rabbi was a staff member for the first time. Rabbi Jaffe said: "The man attends our services on Saturday morning but he goes to attend Mass at a church in Painesville! He's a good Catholic but. . . ."

I really felt sorry for Mr. Whitehill. I liked the man but he seemed so out-of-place at a camp where, among other things, Jewish customs and philosophies were being stressed openly for the first time. It was embarrassing for me to hear counselors and especially the UBY's and other weekend counselors discuss the situation. They felt that something was wrong, although it did not seem to affect the campers. Obviously, it did not take long for word to get back to the Association Board members in town that Mr. Whitehill was "not doing his job." I was worried that something drastic might happen.

Something did happen but not what I had expected. An incident — or rather an epidemic — occurred during the third trip that changed things considerably, and I was glad to see Mr. Whitehill redeem himself. There must have been some kind of food poisoning one night at supper. One by one campers and counselors complained of feeling ill. While very often a case like that becomes hysterically contagious, this time was for real. I was one of the last to succumb to it the following day. Hardly anyone showed up for breakfast the next morning. We called for help from the Painesville Clinic. Counselors could do very little; they were sick, too. For some strange reason, about the only adult who was on his feet and who escaped being ill was Mr. Whitehill. He rose to the occasion in heroic fashion. His physical education training came to the fore as he went from cottage to cottage, ministering, encouraging, and calming the fears of the children. When it was over late that afternoon, he had gained the respect and admiration of the entire camp.

But it was during the Whitehill season that more Jewish content was added to the program. Prior to the opening of camp, Ida Schott had discussed with Rabbi Solomon Goldman koshering the Camp Wise kitchen, specifically with two sets of dishes and cooking utensils and the purchase of kosher meat. Together with the appointment of Rabbi Jaffe to the staff, these two developments represented an even more intensive effort to provide meaningful Jewish content on a regular basis at Camp Wise.

When Whitehill and I said goodbye in August, he told me that he had gone through the strangest season of his life. I never saw the man again, but for me that season led to my next step on the camp ladder. The following year — and again in 1927 — I was appointed director of Camp Wise.

Among my recollections of my first year as director was the addition to staff of Carl Miller, a senior rabbinical student, who turned out to be even more effective than Rabbi Jaffe. His sermons on Friday evenings and Sabbath mornings were much enjoyed, and he was greatly admired by the campers.

I also recall the unique situation that summer in the dining room. The dietician was very insistent that campers eat *everything* on their plates at all meals because the food she would prepare was "good for them." She offered prizes for the best table of campers that would clean their plates. It reached a point where there was great rivalry among tables to win prizes. At one dinner when spinach was on the menu, a counselor, seeing that some campers at his table were leaving some spinach on their plates, told them to pass their plates up to him and he would "clean their plates" so that they would win the prize. He had a voracious appetite! He later became the owner of a large food chain of supermarkets.

One of the most enthusiastic and conscientious counselors of the late 20's and 30's at Camp Wise was Jason Rich. He was a student at Cornell and had never been to Camp Wise. He had known of it, of course, but had not had the chance to visit the camp. He just knew that this new camp was in Painesville. He was called one evening by a member of the Camp Wise Crew and was told that there was a shortage of counselors at Camp Wise. He was asked to report the following morning. He packed a bag in the morning, took the bus to Painesville, and then asked a stranger the location of Camp Wise. The man said it was "just down the road." He first looked for a cab, then decided to walk, not realizing that "just down the road" meant over five miles.

Jason finally arrived in camp that hot morning, exhausted but excited about the prospect of being a counselor. I met him as I was coming out of the library room. He introduced himself and asked what he could do right away. I had no idea that he had just walked from Painesville. As a matter of fact I did not learn of it until that camp season was over. So when he asked what he could do, I said: "See those boys near the recreation hall? They are waiting anxiously for a counselor to take them on a hike." Without a moment's hesitation, Jason Rich asked me to take care of his baggage and ran to the boys. With their guidance he led the campers on a long, long hike — and, of course, back to Camp Wise!

In observing the 20th Anniversary of Camp Wise the summer of 1926, it was decided to make a movie of the activities at camp. The title of the movie was obvious: "A Day at Camp Wise." That movie is still in the archives of the Jewish Community Center. The same script was used as the 20th Anniversary program during the evening of August 15th, which was open to the public: parents, board members, counselors, and newspaper reporters. The uniqueness of the program was the fact that it was all performed around a campfire, with the crowds sitting and standing on the hillsides.

Here are some excerpts taken from a report given by the director at an evening dinner of the Camp Wise Association to commemorate the 20th Anniversary. They illustrate the type of program and activities during this period of the 20's.

> For the first time in many years, there was a noticeable interest in nature lore at camp under the supervision of a specialist in that field, Bert Averbach, a staff member for the entire summer. He took small groups of boys and girls on exploration hikes for the purpose of identifying and becoming familiar with various types of trees, leaves, flowers and birds.
>
> Overnight hikes were as popular as ever. To sleep under the stars and cook breakfast and see a beautiful sunrise were thrills and experiences not soon forgotten. . . . The mother's parties were delightful. Relieved of the responsibilities and care of their babies for one afternoon, the mothers had lunch, played games, sang songs, told stories, and relaxed. How appreciative and thankful they felt at the thought of all the attention showered upon them.
>
> A Camp Wise newspaper, "The Wise Lantern," made its first appearance at the first trip and was followed by one each trip.

A staff of boys and girls chose their own editor, feature writers, and reporters. Julius Sycle was the staff member in charge.

On Friday nights, the Bible pantomimes gave the campers opportunities to portray characters of Jewish history. Episodes in the lives of Moses, Solomon, David, Esther were enacted in dance and song, with beautiful costumes and lighting effects.

These programs were directed by Sadie Siegel, dancing teacher, and Carl Miller, camp Rabbi. . . .

One of the projects, a new Indian Council ring, was built by the older boys in camp, under the ever-watchful eye of George Jackson, the caretaker. The first Sunday of each trip was designated Indian night, and for a few hours the camp took on all the looks and aspects of an Indian reservation. To the beating of tom-toms, young braves and squaws, attired in colorful, appropriate costumes, seated themselves around the Council ring, listened to Indian stories and plays, and performed ceremonial dances. This kind of activity is in line with what other camps around the country are doing in this point in time. The Indian, the original American, had become a folk-hero of the times.

Camp songs this year took on a rather new twist. While certain silly or absurd songs will always have their place in camp, a new type of song, brought back from the Conference at Bear Mountain, New York, such as "Follow the Trail," "Inn of a Starry Sky," and "The Far Northland" became popular. Then, too, parodies of popular songs and songs from recent Broadway shows, "The Vagabond King," "Student Prince," "Toy Shop," and Gilbert and Sullivan lyrics were the songs of the day.

Besides the usual hikes, sports, arts and crafts, swimming, minstrel shows, circus, the UBY's brought out movies every Thursday, an event greatly appreciated. Incidentally, movies were taken to observe the 20th Anniversary of Camp Wise and will be exhibited throughout the neighborhood movie houses in Cleveland.

In 1928 Walter Leo Solomon returned to the Council Educational Alliance as head worker. I had been on the staff of the Alliance as boys' worker from September to June each year since 1923, spending each summer at Camp Wise. Solomon thought I should be on the Alliance staff payroll throughout the year and asked me to direct the three trips for boys at Camp Alliance. Rose Schultz directed the girls' sessions.

Camp Wise Association had allotted 25 acres of land to the Council Educational Alliance in 1924 for a camp for its club members. The land was separated from Camp Wise by a ravine and a creek which formed a natural boundary. A few years later, after the death of Henry Baker, former president of the Alliance, the camp name was changed from Camp Alliance to Camp Henry Baker to honor the memory of the man who contributed so much to the Jewish community in general and to the Alliance in particular. Reluctantly, I left Camp Wise after the 1927 season and went "across the creek" to Camp Alliance in 1928 and 1929. However, I thoroughly enjoyed the more "primitive" type of camping at Camp Alliance, assisted by staff members Hirsh Kaplan and Maurice Englander, and with the help of excellent volunteer leaders.

The Camp Wise staff in these two years (1928 & 1929) was under the supervision of Ruth Schwarzenberg who had been registrar and leader for many years. The rest of the staff included Yetta Kline, girls' worker; Miriam Abramson, assistant girls' worker; Morrie Englander, boys' worker; Elmer Louis, assistant boys' worker; Frank Weinman, camp doctor; Irene Galvin, mothers' worker; and Clara Strauss, nurse. During these two years, Dave Apple, a professional social worker, found his niche in Camp Wise and through all the years into the present has remained a devoted and loyal volunteer: president of the Crew, chairman of the JCC Camp Advisory Committee, and originator of the Case Work-Group Work Study.

At a dinner in honor of Samuel D. Wise at the Chamber of Commerce on May 27, 1931, observing the 25th Anniversary of Camp Wise, this song was sung to the tune of "When Your Hair Has Turned to Silver:"

> Though Sam's hair has turned to silver
> His heart is pure as gold;
> From the lips of laughing children
> His praises shall be told.
>
> While time flows ever swiftly
> Through vales of joy and tears,
> The song of grateful mothers
> Plays softly in his ears.
>
> Not his gifts of gold and silver
> Alone insure his fame,
> But his service to his fellows
> Shall sanctify his name. . . .

Professor Henry M. Busch, guest speaker at this dinner said:

> Summer camps, in teaching children handcrafts of various kinds, build up for many of them hobby activities of a cultural type that can be continued in later years. In teaching children to utilize the out-of-doors and nature study, Camp Wise fulfills an educational ideal in building interests that may last through adult life. In these critical times camp directors and leaders must be aware of their responsibility to conduct camps so as to produce better people for a better world. Camp Wise uses the folklore, songs and dances, crafts and other achievements to enrich the understanding of youngsters about the social world in which they live.

During the Depression years of the 30's and the war years in the 40's,

Albert "Spunk" Kinoy and Sidney Vincent placed their distinctive marks on Camp Wise. Sidney, who went on from public school teaching to become a superb professional community executive, began as a leader in 1935 under Spunk, who was then camp director.

Sidney recalled how the volunteer staff of the 1930's, whose pay consisted of "bed and board," were trained during the off-season months in camping skills and in managing children by the experienced Camp Wise Crew leaders. Before the start of camping sessions, the best of volunteer students were selected to be on staff for a two-week trip. Only permanent staff served for the entire ten weeks of the summer season. Limiting volunteer service to two-week periods created a larger cadre of experienced leaders upon which to draw as needed.

The campers, during Sidney's first years, were primarily from families of limited income, and the depression affected even more of the approximately two hundred youngsters attending each session. But there was now a difference in the program they enjoyed. The objective in earlier years was to provide them with a change away from their restrictive neighborhoods out into fresh air, with wholesome food and sports activities. The camp vacation was designed now to enrich the youngsters' personalities and expose them to more Jewish content, all while exploring the world of nature.

Sidney's first year at Camp Wise was the start of his lifelong friendship with director Albert "Spunk" Kinoy, who was a physical science teacher in New York City. Before going east, he had been a boys' worker in Cleveland at the Woodland Council Educational Alliance, the crowded immigrant area of first settlement. At Camp, Spunk saw his major role as encouraging and directing staff in their hands-on work with their charges. It was a gentle, effective style that put a distinctive stamp on the Kinoy era and ended with our country's entry into the war.

Two other personalities were prominent during Sidney's summer terms at Camp. One was George Jackson, the year-round caretaker of many years, who kept the camp plant in working order, whether with his skilled plumbing, carpentry, or electrical repairs. When necessary, he was also drafted for a baseball game. George was remembered over the years as a living symbol of Camp Wise by thousands of former campers and by the staff as their first and most important asset.

The other figure indelibly linked to Jewish camping in Cleveland for decades was Hugo Mahrer, known affectionately to all as "Uncle Hugo." Without his camping expertise, his love of nature, and his steady years as a community volunteer, Camp Wise would be far less than it is today. The Hugo Mahrer Chapel at the Halle Park site is a reminder of his many contributions and those of his wife, Rose, and of their honored place in the Camp Wise story.

Two major developments in those years, while Sidney was present, had adverse effects on the Camp, which at best could be only partially mitigated. In 1938, the Industrial Rayon Corporation selected a site in Painesville near the Camp for its factory. For the Camp it meant deterioration of the camping grounds, adding to Lake Erie pollution, limiting hiking and outdoor activities to the east, and, when the wind was right (or wrong), spreading the factory smell over the entire area.

Despite its years as a good member of the community, the Camp Wise Association's appeal to be spared a factory neighbor was denied. For Painesville, Industrial Rayon meant jobs, population growth, and tax dollars for the public treasury. The Camp had no choice but to accept the inevitable, and in time, it reached an accommodation with the corporation. During the war years, camp housing facilities were leased in the off season by the corporation for its workers. In return, the Camp gained winterized cabins, shower rooms, and a sizeable contribution to its income budget. But overall, the impact was negative. Camp Wise began to decline physically, and the presence of Industrial Rayon was a smokestack symbol of the difficult years ahead until a new site was found near Burton, Ohio.

Just as the depression ended and Painesville became more urbanized, America's entry into the war created more immediate problems. Spunk Kinoy informed the Association trustees that he had to remain in the New York area and resigned as director. Also during the next several months, many of the older permanent staff went off to war, leaving their positions to be filled by willing but inexperienced high school seniors. Many of the resulting wartime problems were overcome and camp went on, with the perseverance of the staff and the determination of the Camp trustees and supporters. The years 1942 and 1943 were sparked by Sidney, who took on major responsibility for programming and administration.

Still another change was an end to the rivalry with Camp Henry Baker, the summer camp of the Council Educational Alliance, across a small ravine from Camp Wise. Friendly competition went on every season not only between the two groups of campers but also between the staffs, divisions with perceived differences in social background and professional training. On both informal scales Camp Baker was rated higher by some. They were certainly different but one was not necessarily better than the other. Camp Baker was run, since its establishment in the 1920's, by a professional CEA staff — me, for one, in 1928 and 1929. In 1943, perhaps because of wartime limitations in resources and personnel, the two camps were merged under the Camp Wise name to be administered by the CEA with the Camp Wise Association as trustees. This arrangement remained in force until 1948, when the Association was dissolved and title to the assets it had held since 1907 was transferred to the newly established Jewish Community Center.

Camp Wise Association

As we delve into the history of Camp Wise during the first two decades, there are two names in particular that are mentioned over and over again. In addition to Samuel D. Wise and Eugene Geismer, the founders of the camp, the two individuals whose contributions toward the success of Camp Wise stand out above the rest are Ida Schott and William Treuhaft. As to volunteer leaders, too numerous to list, Dave Warshawsky started as a young helper in 1907 and continued through his adult life into the 50's and 60's as a devoted leader. In the 20's and 30's, Henry Marcuson and Leon Weil played prominent roles in every capacity, as leaders, board members, and officers of the Camp Wise Crew and the Association, as did Hugo Mahrer in later years.

In the operation of the camp from the start and, in fact, for at least the first twenty years or so, the volunteer counselors were the ones whose contributions were the greatest of any made in its development. There was such an unbelievable, keen desire on the part of the young Jewish men and women to come to camp as leaders. Even the arduous tasks of opening and closing camp were for many years done almost solely by these volunteers.

At the first meeting of the Camp Wise Association on November 25th, 1907, at the Temple, we find listed the pioneer Board members: Rabbi Louis Wolsey, Samuel Wise, Rabbi Moses Gries, Dr. Isadore Grossman, Meyer Weil, Bella Wiener, Lillian Grossman, Beatrice Moss, Lillian [Lily] Sloss, Molly Stearn, Ida Schott, and Eugene Geismer, the first president of the Association. The Association minutes record many events and developments in the history of Camp Wise, illustrated by the following excerpts:

1928

> Motion by Mrs. Rothenberg, seconded by Dr. Markey, to approve the following scale of fees for 1928:
>
> Children under 3 years ....$1.00 per trip (two weeks)
> Children 3 to 5 years ....$3.00   "   "
> Children 6 to 12 years ....$4.00   "   "
> Children 13 to 16 and over....$6.00   "   "
> Mothers ....$7.00   "   "

1934

> George Mayer made a motion, seconded by Henry Marcuson, to appoint a committee with Judge Lewis Drucker as chairman to study the possibilities of introducing more Jewish content into the programs.

1936

> The City Ice Inspector was out to examine the refrigerator. He found the following things lacking: (1) gaskets on all doors; (2) outside door is warped; (3) it is too small for a normal size piece of ice. The ice must therefore be chipped before going through the door.

Two reports from two Program Directors of Camp Wise within two years reveal the shift in programs and the gradual efforts to implement the desired "Jewish content" in camp activities. Frances Hoffman, who was the Program Director in the war year of 1944, said: "After clean-up in the morning, the campers are off to the woods or the craft shop as Indians, Commandos, Hawaiians, Chinese, Mexicans, often complete with costumes they had made themselves. . ."

The following year, Bernice Teitelbaum, Program Director, said: "Our objectives assume a broader scope than fun and games and outdoor living. Through discussion, music, dancing and dramatics, Sabbath observances, and other channels, we try to develop in the children a deeper appreciation and understanding of their Jewishness, their Jewish heritage. We also want them to accept and understand peoples of other groups. However, this *is* a Jewish camp, under Jewish auspices, and primarily for Jewish children."

The post-war years brought about significant changes in attitudes toward Jewish identification in Jewish community centers and Jewish summer camps. The National Jewish Welfare Board undertook a survey, directed by Dr. Oscar Janowsky, "to guide it in the development of a post-war program." Dr. Janowsky expressed concern about those workers in centers and camps who conduct face-to-face activities and "are sadly lacking in qualifications to conduct Jewish programs." He aroused some critical reaction but also stimulated thinking about the whole subject of appropriate Jewish background in training programs.

After much discussion during the years prior to and shortly after the founding of the State of Israel, the Board of the Camp Wise Association and the Jewish Community Center reported in 1948 to the Jewish community:

> Camp Wise is conducted by the Jewish community to promote the adjustment of the Jewish children of Cleveland by providing a wholesome, happy educational experience in the out-of-doors for the maximum number of Cleveland Jewish young people. Camp Wise seeks to achieve its purpose through a program of activities to serve the general needs of its children for physical and social growth as well as to meet their Jewish needs.
>
> On the accomplishment of this latter purpose, it operates according to kosher dietary regulations, plans extensive weekly Jewish Sabbath observance for Friday evenings and Saturday, selects camp staff competent to serve particular Jewish needs based upon Jewish history, background, culture and modern Jewish problems. Since the creation of the State of Israel, Jewish camps — Camp Wise included — have incorporated Hebrew songs, dances, Hebrew villages in their programs.

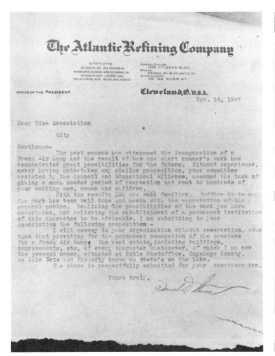

Samuel D. Wise letter conveying property (Stein's on the Lake) to the Camp Wise Association. (E)

Samuel D. Wise posing on fender of his Packard at the camp named for him, 1908. (A)

Some Camp Wise leaders — Samuel D. Wise at left, Buck Warshawsky next to bugler Charlie Dietz, 1908. (I)

A visit to Camp Wise, Interurban Stop 133, ca. 1915. (C)

View of section for mothers with babies on Sunday visitors' day, ca. 1915. (C)

Delivering duckboard flooring for UBY's tent, 1911. (C)

A visit to Camp Wise by Walter Leo Solomon, Council Educational Alliance director, ca 1915. (D)

David Warshawsky at camp, 1908. (H)

Oscar Markey, camp director, 1920-21. (G)

Grace Grossman, camp director, 1922-1924. (C)

Volunteer young adult camp leaders; David Warshawsky standing, ca. 1917. (C)

UBY's leaders in front of their cabin; David Sheinbart, Leon Weil, Eli Drucker, Saul Drucker, Moe Gimp, ca. 1921.
(C)

Leaders posing informally on the beach. Standing: Grace Grossman, Florence Printz, Mickey Weitz, Natalie Biederman Steuer, Babette Devay; kneeling: Al Brown, Claire Feldman, Bea Feniger (face covered), 1922. (B)

A July 4th celebration at camp. Volunteers posing with Samuel D. Wise at left, ca. 1910. (C)

The main building at Camp Wise; first floor, dining and recreation room; second floor, sleeping quarters for boys and director, ca. 1918. (C)

Dinner time. At rear right, Alex Warshawsky, 1910. (C)

Nymphs dancing at a camp entertainment, 1915. (H)

Working-class boys from the Woodland neighborhood in the first year of Camp Wise, 1908. (I)

Mothers with infant children during a 1911 camp trip. (C)

Choosing up sides. At right, Buck Warshawsky, 1908. (I)

On the Camp Wise cliff, including Dave Warshawsky, center, with volunteer beauties, 1908. (I)

A Lake Erie session in swimming costumes of yesteryear, 1908. (I)

Posing on the beach during a swim break. Note some shaved heads, 1908. (I)

Policing the camp grounds, 1908. (I)

On tiptoe for a drink of water. No question about his pleasure at a break from his old neighborhood, ca. 1920. (C)

Boys and volunteer leaders on the swings. Note the contrast in their dress, 1911. (C)

Airing the bedding in front of the boys' quarters for the next trip, 1908. (I)

Ring-around-the-roses, 1908. (I)

A Model T carful of camp leaders, ca. 1922. On the running board, Harry Weinberg and Henry Marcuson. (B)

Campers, leaders, and a kite frame. The leaders at the back: Harry Weinberg, Grace Grossman, and Al Brown, 1922. (B)

Girl campers surrounding their leader, 1908. (I)

Girl campers at play in front of the main building, ca. 1915. (C)

Young adult volunteers in front of the UBY's tent, 1911. (C)

The O'lovus rival tent with its volunteers and a group of campers, 1911. (C)

World War II Years at Camp Wise — 1942 to 1945

Like all other summer camps, both private and institutional, Camp Wise had its difficulties during the war years, but the camp seasons continued and prevailed. Despite the war-time restrictions and young men going into service, the Board of the Camp Wise Association never wavered in its desire to give the children and mothers the best possible camp experience. Women leaders were in the majority in 1943-44. Deborah Miller was camp director, under the supervision of Hugo Mahrer, chairman of the camp committee, and aided by the volunteer services of Sid Vincent as consultant.

In 1942, Spunk Kinoy, as noted, could no longer continue as camp director because of wartime school teaching requirements in New York. Sid Vincent also had to turn down the offer to direct the camp, and Harold Tannenbaum was appointed director in 1942. It was suggested that because of the shortage of men volunteer leaders for the two-week trips, a few of the better leaders might stay on for the entire summer and be paid $25 to $30 for the season. This was an important innovation because it was the first time that the Association Board thought about paying leaders instead of asking them to volunteer their services. This idea — with a much higher pay scale — became the Camp Wise policy by the mid-40's, and there was no further need of a Camp Wise Crew.

Lil Berkowitz was the last president of the Crew (1943-44). Others during the last 15 years were: Henry Marcuson, 1930; Hugo Mahrer, 1932; Leon Weil, 1933; Henry Kutash, 1934; Dave Apple, 1935-36; Norman Gutfeld, 1937-38; Ruth Kline, 1939-40; and Elmoe Goldberg, 1941-42. The Camp Wise Crew had played a great part and performed a remarkable volunteer service for 30 years at Camp Wise. End of an era!

In September, 1943, after the camp season ended, Sanford Solender, executive director of the Council Educational Alliance, whose responsibilities included the evaluation of the camp program, praised the outstanding contributions of Sidney Vincent, Hugo Mahrer, Deborah Miller, Lil Berkowitz, George Hays, and the Camp Wise Crew. He pointed out that it was only the efforts of these individuals that permitted the camp to have a successful season in what otherwise would have been insurmountable war-time difficulties.

In 1943, George H. Hays, president of the Camp Wise Association, and Meyer T. Wolpaw, president of the Council Educational Alliance, agreed in principle to a merger of Camp Wise and Camp Henry Baker. The latter would be known as West Camp Wise, with emphasis on a more primitive type of camping program for older boys and girls.

That same year, and also in 1944, there were feature newspaper stories about "*SOMETHING NEW FOR CAMPERS AT CAMP WISE*" — "*TEEN-AGE CROP CORPS HELPS WAR EFFORT.*" According to an article in the *Plain Dealer*, "65 members (14-16 years of age) of the Crop Corps of Camp Wise are giving willing and indispensable help to the farmers of the neighborhood, doing an outstanding war-time job." Howard Robbins, camp staff member and originator of the Crop Corps, having been honorably discharged from the army, wrote the former commanding officer of his regiment: "The campers leave at 8:00 a.m. and return about 4:30 p.m. For the first time in their lives they ride behind a horse, run a cultivator, drive a tractor and, more important, they feel they are doing something for their country during such a critical period in history." His commanding officer replied: "I know of no finer work that you and those campers could be doing. Keep up the good work." The Crop Corps' contribution to the home front war effort was officially recognized by the Federal government.

III.
CAMP WISE IN
HALLE PARK, BURTON, OHIO
1966 —

The Jewish community had been aware for many years of the serious inadequacies of the camp location in Painesville, Ohio. Although first indicated officially in the "Self-Study of the Jewish Community Center" in 1953, the situation at the camp had been brought to the attention of the Camp Wise Board by staff members Spunk Kinoy and Sid Vincent as far back as the mid-30's.

To recapitulate, there were good reasons for the decision to relocate: (1) increased pollution of the lake; (2) air pollution by the acrid fumes from the Industrial Rayon plant across the road; (3) noise and traffic in front of the main area of the camp; (4) loss of hiking area because the Rayon plant had been built on the grounds where overnight hikes were held; (5) loss of privacy due to the housing settlement at Sunset Point; and (6) erosion of the beach.

For five years, from 1953 to 1958, an ad hoc camp committee of the JCC searched for a new site on which to relocate the Painesville camp. In 1953, at the request of the Jewish Community Federation, an outline of the requirements for a new resident camp facility had been drawn up and submitted by the camp committee. During the next five years, the committee conducted its search for the new site. As a result of that search, a good potential site of 325 acres near Burton, Ohio, in Geauga County, was located in 1958.

I remember attending a meeting at the home of George Hays in 1958, where a group called "Friends of Camp Wise" agreed to purchase this site in order to sell it at cost to the Jewish Community Center when it became ready to acquire this new location for the camp.

Because the "Friends of Camp Wise" performed such an important service at a critical period, their names should be recorded in this chronicle: Art Dettelbach, Chairman of the Camp Development Committee; Irv Ballonoff, Chairman of the Day Camp Committee; George Goulder, President of the JCC; Herman Eigen, Executive Director of the JCC; and Abe Bonder, Camp Director during this period. Others included: Dave Apple, Nate Berman, Ernie Brody, Jac Fallenberg, Max Friedman, Art Hirsch, Julie Kravitz, Harold Krawitz, Sam Levine, Hugo Mahrer, Mort Mandel, Ernie Siegler, Dave Warshawsky, Harry Wolpaw, and Sam Zelvy. The legal work of the sale was taken care of pro bono by Dan Loeser and Larry Williams.

At a meeting in 1963, Art Dettelbach explained to the group that it had become necessary to complete the sale without delay because the Painesville site had been sold to the Cleveland Electric Illuminating Company with the stipulation that Camp Wise move at the close of the 1965 season. The proceeds of the sale — $350,000 —would be sufficient to meet a major share of the cost of the new camp site. But much more would be needed to build a new camp.

Just as the Jewish community was blessed in 1907 when Samuel D. Wise

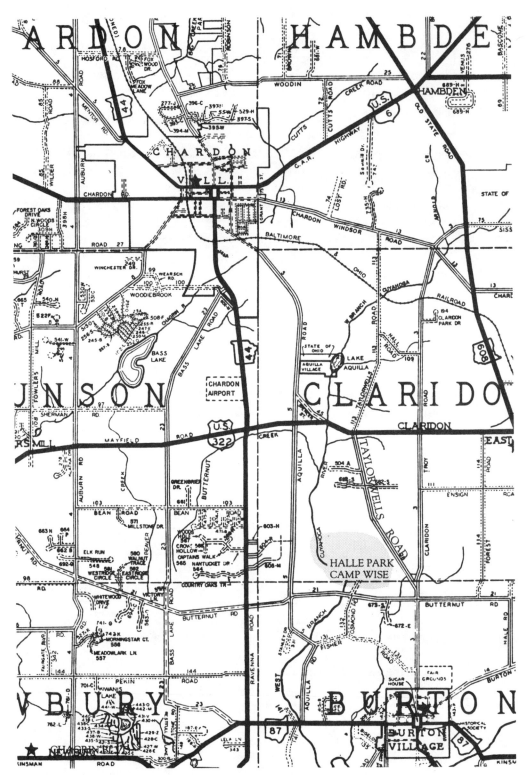

Halle Park — Camp Wise, 1966 - Burton, Ohio, Geauga County. County Engineers Office, 1987.

made possible the first camping facility at Stop 133, Lake Shore Boulevard, so was the Jewish community blessed again through the generosity of Eugene and Blanche Halle. Mr. and Mrs. Halle were well known for their interest in civic, educational, and philanthropic enterprises. With Philmore J. Haber, attorney for the Halle family, acting as advisor to the Cleveland Foundation for the Halle Fund, a grant of $300,000 from that fund was made available, enabling the consolidation of all camping activities of the JCC in one large, parklike setting. Thus, the Eugene and Blanche Halle Park became the new home of Camp Wise and also of the JCC [John] Anisfield Day Camp.

For accomplishing this change of camp sites and later following up on all the details of the opening in Burton, much credit should be given to the Camp Steering Committee, which after five years completed its work in 1966. In addition to Art Dettelbach, Chairman, the Committee included Irv Ballonoff, Ernie Siegler, Herman Eigen, and Abe Bonder.

Herman Eigen was Executive Director of the Jewish Community Center from 1954 to 1976, the period during which the JCC was built on Mayfield and the new Camp Wise opened in Burton. Both of these projects required skillful coordination of the professional staff and lay committees. The Cleveland Jewish community was indeed fortunate to have had Herman Eigen as the executive of the JCC in this critical period in its history.

Abe Bonder, who had been an expert camp consultant for the National Jewish Welfare Board in New York, played a most important role in the planning and building of the camp in Burton. In fact, Abe Bonder above all others left his personal imprint on the new Camp Wise. The layout of the buildings and grounds was his dream, and he lived to see that dream come true. He had been director of Camp Wise from 1953, much longer than any other director. He had a national reputation in the camping field, and development of the camp in Burton became the high point of his distinguished career for which he will be long remembered.

The 325 acres of virgin woodland which comprise Halle Park have made possible a much expanded nature and campcraft program. A basic purpose of Camp Wise has always been to provide a creative educational experience in group living in the outdoors. Campers get a first-hand knowledge of the natural world outside the city. Long hikes in the woods, singing "around the campfire, 'neath the stars so bright, we have met in comradeship tonight" (the start of a camp song) provide memories to last a lifetime.

The creation of the Leon G. Weil Nature Trail, through the generosity of Elizabeth and William C. Treuhaft, is another resource which instills in campers a sense of appreciation of and respect for the outdoors and for all living things. At the dedication in 1979, the following tribute was read:

> This Trail is appropriately dedicated to the memory of the late Leon G. Weil, whose interest in Camp Wise started in the early 20's when he served as a volunteer counselor, and later as President for many years, of the Camp Wise Association. He was one of the prime movers, in 1948, of the plan to merge Camp

Wise into the newly organized Jewish Community Center. This Nature Trail, a living memorial to Leon Weil, will serve as a classroom, exhibiting various aspects of botany, zoology, geology and ecology to enhance appreciation for the relationship between campers and their natural environment. It is hoped that campers will continue to use and further develop this Trail for years to come.

Of the many activities at the camp in Burton which illustrate the great change from the early years, most important is the commitment to Jewish content and programming that now characterizes the camp. An environment of Jewish living has been created throughout the camp. Weekly Shabbat programs held in the Hugo Mahrer Outdoor Chapel are planned by the campers. Jewish and Israeli folk music and dance increase campers' awareness of their Jewish culture and heritage. Through this carefully programmed combination of camp activities with Jewish concepts and values, children discover — some perhaps for the first time — the joy of being Jewish. There is a definite sense of Jewish living at Camp Wise in Burton.

The achievement of these distinctive Jewish goals in programming calls for a camp staff that is equipped to promote, develop, and guide these programs. At Camp Wise there is a careful recruitment of counselors who have a Jewish background and interests. A list of directors of the camp since the mid-40's is a reflection of the emphasis on Jewish purposes in the programs: Lil Berkowitz, Debbie Miller, Irwin Gold (before retirement, executive director of the Toronto Jewish Congress), Murray Raim, Sol Green, Hy Tabachnik (now executive director, Akron JCC), Abe Bonder, Marv Goldish, Leonard Rubin, Ami Nahshon (now executive vice president, Jewish Federation of the Greater East Bay, Oakland, Cal.), Barbara Wohlworth, Paul Sack, Scott Brown, Michelle Vernon, Karin Hess, and the present director, Lynne Leutenberg.

The presence of *shlichim* (Israeli cultural emissaries) and representatives of the Israeli Scout movement further strengthens the Jewish identification at the camp. Supervisors, specialists, and counselors are chosen on the basis of their experience and skill in working with children, but also on their Jewish background.

Using actual program facts and figures of the 1988 season as an example, here is a picture of the Camp Wise of today. In 1988, there were two camp trips:

> 4 weeks from June 21 to July 19
> 3 weeks from July 24 to August 14
> Camp capacity per trip was 180 campers.
>
> Camp is organized by age groups into villages:
> Kfar Chalutzim .... 3rd-4th-5th Graders
> Kfar Ohalim .... 6th and 7th Graders
> Kfar Noar .... 8th and 9th Graders
> Kfar Solel .... 10th Graders

A cabin group consists of 8 to 10 campers per cabin. The size of the specialty group varies, depending on camp program.

Kfar Chalutzim, the *Pioneer Village*, houses the youngest campers, for many of them the first time they are away from home. They select their outdoor activities under the guidance of experienced counselors.

Kfar Ohalim, the *Tent Village*, houses campers in specially designed semi-cabins as part of the rustic setting of this village. A separate recreation hall with a fireplace adds to the high village spirit.

Kfar Noar is the *Teen Village*, where campers share a growing world of ideas. Activities vary from sharpening individual skills, as in athletics or dramatics, to group evening programs and an extended canoe trip.

Kfar Solel, the *Trailblazers*, offers activities and experiences to meet the campers' sense of independence and responsibility. They have their own evening volley ball, tennis, and out-of-camp events, such as longer trips, water skiing, and other challenging opportunities.

Taken from the fact sheet at Halle Park Open House in 1986:

Swimming: Camp Wise has a 25-yard, heated, L-shaped swimming pool supervised by certified Red Cross lifeguards and instructors. Beginning, intermediate, and advanced swimming, basic rescue, and water safety are taught.

Arts and Crafts: Different art materials, including yarn, textiles, wood, clay, and natural resources from the camp's surroundings are used creatively by campers individually and in groups in the campcrafts building.

Sports: Softball, football, basketball, soccer, and tennis are some of the popular games played on the camp's large athletic fields. All campers participate in a group trail ride on horseback. Clinics led by top amateur and professional athletes are a highlight of the sports program.

Campcraft and *Nature Lore*: Campfire programs, overnight camping, cookouts, and hiking are activities using the natural surroundings of the camp. Campers study ecology and learn to identify trees, animals, and insects on the Leon G. Weil Nature Trail. They grow flowers and vegetables in the camp garden.

Drama: The Camp Wise Theatre has a fully equipped, theatrically lighted stage. The play presentation by each village is a highlight of the camp season.

Jewish Program: An environment of Jewish living is created throughout the camp. Weekly Shabbat programs planned by campers are held in the Hugo Mahrer Outdoor Chapel. The presence of *shlichim* and of *tsofim* (Israeli scouts) deepens campers knowledge and awareness of Israel and our Jewish heritage.

Finances: In 1988, camp fees for JCC members averaged about $250 per week:

   For the 4 weeks trip: $1,000 (non-members $1,285)
   For the 3 weeks trip: $755 (non-members $970)
   Additional fees for optional specialties, such as horseback riding and tennis.

Income, in addition to campers' fees, comes from scholarships donated by Alliwise, National Council of Jewish Women, Cleveland Section, and the Jewish Community Federation.

Meals are nutritionally balanced, kosher food served "family style" in the dining room. Special snacks are served before bedtime.

Family weekends are held after the regular camp season.

Camp Wise strives to create a friendly and cooperative atmosphere in which each camper may grow and develop. This has been its creed and philosophy since it was founded in 1907.

A FINAL WORD

This has been a tale of three sites in three cities — Euclid, Painesville, and Burton. Camp Wise has achieved an assured place in the hearts and minds of a number of generations of Jewish children and adults. A record of 82 years of Camp Wise should include an estimated figure of the number of campers in all those years. Here it is:

   At the Euclid site, Stop 133, Lake Shore Boulevard, from 1907 to 1924, the camp capacity was approximately 150 for each of the five trips, two weeks each trip, during the summer — 750 campers a season or 12,750 for the seventeen years.

   At the second site, in Painesville, from 1924 to 1965, the capacity was 200 campers for each of the five trips — 1,000 for each season — or a total of 42,000 for those 42 years.

   At the third site, in Burton, from 1966 to 1983. Three trips of three weeks each with approximately 500 campers each season, or about 9,000 for these eighteen years. Starting in 1984, there were two trips, one of four weeks and a second of three weeks, for a total of 1,765 campers for the last five years.

   Thus, give or take a few hundred, it would seem fairly

accurate to say that the number of campers served from 1907 through 1988 would approximate the incredible total of more than 65,000 children. This figure does not include the 40 years of Alliwise, average about 100 each year. Nor does it include the use of Camp Wise before and after the regular camping seasons by other organizations, such as Mothers Clubs, JCC youth groups, family weekends, temple and synagogue conclaves, and religious retreats.

Starting with mothers and babies, even in 1907, Camp Wise has provided a wonderful holiday for adults, including the older adults. It has always proved to be an enriching experience, contributing to their sense of well-being, broadening their leisure time skills and, most important, helping them make new friends.

As for camp fees — in the early years they were at a bare minimum. The first fees were 50 cents a week for those who could afford to pay that amount. Later, the fees rose to 75 cents, then to $1.25, $3.00, $5.00 a trip, and up to $17 to $20 for two weeks in the late 40's and early 50's.

As the camp philosophy and policies changed from a settlement house fresh-air camp to a more modern and sophisticated concept, emphasizing Jewishness and Jewish living, with paid staff members (instead of volunteers), many of them specialists in various camping activities, such as horse-back riding, tennis, canoeing, campcrafts, dramatics, and other programs, the fees had to be adjusted in accordance with the increased costs of operating the camp at the high standards expected. There are, it should be noted, scholarships and a sliding scale for those who cannot afford the full fee. Although Camp Wise is a Jewish camp with Jewish purposes, as a United Way agency it serves the entire community and no child is ever denied admission to Camp Wise solely because of lack of funds.

The Camp Wise Story is one without an ending but will continue for years to come, bringing the joys of comradeship and the pleasures of nature to many more generations of campers. For me it was a pleasure and privilege to have shared in its history.

David Warshawsky (1894-1989) was a younger brother of Abel "Buck" Warshawsky, first head leader of boys at Camp Wise in 1908. David enrolled as a camper in 1908 with their mother's consent and Buck's promise of close supervision. It was the start of his enthusiastic commitment to Camp Wise as a volunteer, member of the Camp Wise Association, and trustee of the Council Educational Alliance and its successor, the Jewish Community Center. He received special recognition for these decades of service at the dedication ceremonies of Halle Park, where Camp Wise relocated in 1966. He readily admitted that he had received as much as he had given throughout his long involvement in the camping and Jewish Center movement.

In his manuscript autobiography David included a chapter describing his early experiences at Camp Wise. He made a special point of recalling his sensitive awareness of the economic and social distinctions between the campers, sons of recent immigrants from Eastern Europe, and their leaders, most of them scions of Cleveland's established, Americanized, German-Jewish families.

This excerpt from David's manuscript was edited and is printed here with the permission of his wife, Florence Warshawsky.

Early Days
at
Camp Wise

David Warshawsky

I remember well the summer of 1908. I spent every morning at the playground of the Council Educational Alliance, and about noon I would head for my corner at East Ninth and Euclid, to arrive about two o'clock and begin my work selling newspapers. Sam, an older brother, then in his junior year at high school, had outgrown his job as a newsboy. He had secured a job as a copy boy at the *Cleveland News* for the summer.

My brother, Abel, known to all as "Buck," had been working at the C.E.A. playground, but this particular summer he was appointed head boys' leader at Camp Wise, which had opened the previous summer.

Buck suggested that I go along with him to Camp Wise for a two-week period. I had never been away from home overnight, and my mother, who was uninformed about the Camp, objected at first. But Buck reassured her by explaining that it would give me an opportunity to have a fine, healthful vacation in the country and maybe put on some weight. Thus I obtained parental consent.

This meant that after July 4, when I was booked to join the first group of campers, I would have to give up my newspaper business for the two weeks at camp.

The printed instructions suggested that each camper bring a grip or some similar container with three changes of underwear, three changes of outer wear, two pairs of shoes or tennis sneakers, a tooth brush, toilet articles, and soap and three towels. I placed my belongings in an old leather satchel that I had borrowed. They consisted of the necessary under garments, a pair of overalls, two white shirts, a cap, toilet articles, and a prayer book. I had to promise that I would "daven," say my prayers, every morning. I didn't. Neither did Buck. In fact, I don't remember whether he had even learned how to read Hebrew or knew the prayers by rote or what they meant.

The great day of departure finally arrived and all the children, ages six to fourteen, gathered outside the C.E.A. building awaiting the special car that was to take us to Camp Wise on the lake shore, some fifteen miles east of Cleveland.

Miss Hilda Mulhauser, who was in charge of admissions, was to accompany us to Camp. I knew her very well. In fact, it was she who suggested to Buck that I become a camper also. Miss Mulhauser, who appeared to us over six feet tall, was a round, buxom woman with an all-embracing heart, and she was a fount of all wisdom. She loomed above the children and their mothers, who surrounded her like chicks around a mother hen. The anxious mothers hovered over their youngsters and asked countless questions of poor, patient Hilda Mulhauser, who never failed at being sympathetic, kind and understanding. Even though Abel was with the group, I had a few qualms—but not for long.

Many of the children's belongings were brought in baskets. Very few had satchels or grips or leather containers. There were more tears among the parents than among the children when they began to enter the huge red interurban car. A few of the little ones ran back to the curb, before the bus started, for a final hug, but Miss Mulhauser mothered them back. Like me, almost none of them had been away from their parents before for any length of time. Some were recent immigrant arrivals who could not yet converse in anything but their mother tongue, Yiddish.

I managed to find a seat by the window and waved to those who were there to see me off until they were out of sight. Miss Mulhauser, Buck, and eight of the counselors, four girls and four boys, accompanied us. They quickly started a songfest and within a short while the children joined in and forgot their fears and tears and began to sing. When we passed the city limits, we became engrossed with the countryside. Cold lemonade, cookies, and popcorn were passed around.

The trip in the large red interurban car was a new experience for most of the children. Many of them had not ranged far beyond the Jewish streets in which they lived.

The main road to Euclid from Cleveland was unpaved in those early days, over sixty years ago. At Shoreline Stop No. 133, we were met by several counselors, then called leaders, and a decrepit looking horse and wagon. The driver was a gaunt man named Charlie Dietz, who proved to be invaluable as a gardener, plumber, kitchen helper, farmer, and musician, as well as a baseball filler-in at the Camp.

The luggage was loaded into the wagon and we all marched down the long road into Camp Wise. The leaders and Miss Mulhauser headed the procession while Buck followed at the tailend. Soon before us loomed a huge wooden building that looked like a barracks. The upstairs proved to be the boys' sleeping quarters, and the first floor housed the dining room and kitchen. I still can savor the pleasant odor of toast and coffee that rose from the kitchen the next morning. A wide porch surrounded the building on three sides. A huge grass-covered field greeted us at the end of the walk. To the left, along its entire length and ending above the lake, was a path alongside the eight small wooden cottages for the girl campers. Each cottage housed four girls and one of the girl leaders. The male leaders for the boys occupied their own separate cottage to the right of the main wooden building. Above the cliff was a grove of beautiful trees that partially obscured the glistening lake below.

Charlie Dietz together with some of the older counselors unloaded the childrens' luggage from the wagon, while the children lined up for a quick checkup. After this, we boys were led to the second floor of the main building and assigned three to a room. Each room was furnished with three cots, a dresser, and a chair, a truly monastic setting. The girls were assigned to their cottages by their leaders.

I was to share Buck's room at the top of the stairs, with the strict understanding that because he was my brother and head leader did not imply that I would have any special privileges. I was subjected to all the same rules and regulations that all the other camp kids followed. In fact, Buck insisted that I toe the line much more rigidly than the others. After the upstairs visit, we were directed to the men's lavatory and washroom outside, some fifty feet from the building, to clean up for lunch. Ten minutes later a loud bugle call announced that lunch was ready. Charlie Dietz was the bugler, and thereafter for each meal he would blow a tune to summon the hungry. The next morning and each morning thereafter, at 6:30, we were awakened by his brassy morning reveille.

The dining room was a large rectangular space with six tables evenly spaced along both walls. Each table seated twelve, five on a side, plus a child on the end and a leader at the head. After the seating, Mr. Geismer, who was president of the Camp, arose and greeted all of us. Then one of the children stood up and spoke a simple blessing, which he first gave in Hebrew and then translated into English: "Blessed art Thou, our Lord, King of the universe, who bringest forth bread from the Earth."

After lunch, Mr. Geismer announced that everyone should bring down his luggage, whether in a basket, grip, or satchel, to be examined. Apparently some of the parents had doubts about the food and had included various types of kosher cooking carefully wrapped and hidden in between their clothing. Each child had to lay whatever food he had in his luggage on the dining room table. The food was to be shared with everyone in the entire group who wanted any part of it, and whatever remained uneaten was to be tossed out.

The lunch was simple. It consisted of borsht, bread and butter, hard boiled eggs, milk in quantity, and fruit for dessert. The meals that followed were all kosher, since most of the children came from Orthodox homes. No child ever left the table hungry during the two weeks that I was there. We had fish and vegetables at noon, cereal in the morning, all the milk we could drink, and all the bread and butter we wanted. But never meat and milk or butter at the same meal.

The first night the leaders joined the boys when they went upstairs to sleep and examined their clothing. It was a revelation to learn that many of them had never slept between sheets. I don't believe any, or a few at the most, had pajamas or night gowns. Some had an extra set of underwear for sleeping only. Most of them planned to sleep in the same sweaty underwear they had worn all day. Apparently they had never known anything different. Those who were especially dirty were obliged to go down to the washroom and clean up as much as they could before returning to their beds. To those who had no extra underwear or sleeping garments, the leaders suggested that they sleep naked. This did not seem to bother them. The weather fortunately was very hot.

The boys in each room appointed their own captains. They were responsible for a thorough room sweeping in the morning, for the orderly manner in which their clothes were hung, and for the neatness of their beds. The next morning the leaders were busy teaching the boys how to make their beds and turn the corners at the bottom. At the Sunday noon dinner, prizes were awarded to the boys whose rooms were the neatest for that week. The prize was a man-sized piece of pie for each member of the winning room, and a badge.

That first night a number of homesick young ones cried. In each case, one of the older girl leaders would come and comfort him. After the second night, this was no longer a problem. It didn't take long for the children to feel at home, and after the first day's exhausting activities, they went to sleep very quickly. It became the custom for the counselors to stay up at least an hour or two after the children were in bed. Sometimes they would have a snack in the kitchen of some of the goodies they had brought out for themselves.

This was the experimental beginning of Camp Wise. It was apparent from the start that there was no organized program. The founders and leaders were feeling their way to become acquainted with the children and to learn what would make them happiest with the limited budget on hand. The fee was $.50 a week per child, but where that might have offered a hardship, there was no charge at all. After being awakened by Charlie's reveille in the morning, the daring ones who braved the morning chill would put on their bathing suits, and in a line behind Buck, would snake their way back and forth across the field to the top of the cliff, then descend the stairs into the cove which served as our beach. A quick dive into the water, five minutes of splashing or swimming, and then we would scramble up the stairs again to snake-line across the field back to our rooms, thoroughly awake and with appetites sharpened for breakfast.

After breakfast the first morning, all of the children were advised that they would be given a brief physical examination by Dr. Grossman, who each week that summer volunteered his services and lived at the Camp. After the examination, each child was sent to Mrs. Morgan, who was a volunteer, for a head examination. She was called our "head worker" and was well known as a masseuse and hairdresser. The girls came first, and after their hair was washed, they would sit in the sun where the leaders would entertain them and tell them stories until their hair was dry enough to be combed.

Several of the older campers stood by to help carry out Dr. Grossman's orders. At least two out of three boys had their hair clipped, not necessarily because their heads contained any live objects, but because, as Doc expressed it, it was healthy for their heads to absorb two weeks of fresh air and sun. Surprising how thickly their hair grew back, and how much easier it was to keep clean. This decisive move was even ordered for me, and together we all looked like a group of young convicts racing around the camp. I usually wore nothing but a black gym shirt, a pair of overalls, and black rubber-soled sneakers, and my outfit was about par for the course.

After these preliminaries, the day's fun began. There never was any difficulty in starting a ball game. This was the sure way of keeping most of us happily busy. Time passed very quickly. We went swimming just before lunch and in the late afternoon just before supper, if we chose. Each Thursday morning Charlie's wagon was loaded with baskets of sandwiches, milk, ice tea, and fruit and sometimes a treat from one of the counselors, and we would march down Bliss Road, which was still unpaved and lined with farms on both sides. Charlie knew the farmers in the area and always arranged beforehand for a place to camp and stop for lunch. We would follow the leaders, singing from the time we left until we stopped. There was a kindly farmer who invited us to come any time and offered to furnish water and anything else that would be of help. His farm was about two miles from Camp, and usually it was noon when we arrived at the site, tired and eager for lunch. Usually we returned to camp in the late afternoon in time for a swim. The leaders planned many pleasant events during the week, but the most enjoyable was the campfire at night on the cliff overlooking the lake. Here everyone joined in singing, and story telling by the children as well as the counselors was encouraged. As a rule, there would be popcorn balls or watermelon in season or ice cream as treats provided by the counselors or friends of the Camp. Time and again some of the youngsters would be asleep before the "Good Night Ladies" was sung.

During those two weeks, my eyes were opened to the realization of the small, limited world in which I had been living. The leaders, all older than I, came from a totally different economic background. Each one was chosen because he or she had had some experience with social work, and almost all of them were attending college or were graduates aiming at the kind of higher education that I had dreamt of but would not realize. They lived in the areas where the more affluent families had settled years before. Their parents may have been immigrants, but all of them were born here and thoroughly Americanized. They all were Jewish, but few if any of them were Orthodox. Several of them were junior members of a plush country club in the city. The leaders ranged from about eighteen to twenty-one, and it was apparent that all of them had had some experience in handling children. Some were camp veterans at private summer camps in the past, and three had been counselors while attending college. A few were girl counselors. Most of them had been to modern camps in New England

and were experienced in campcraft and trained in methods to keep boys and girls happily busy even on rainy days. Several played tennis, and it wasn't long before nearby tennis courts had been located.

Their views on life, their scope, their way of living, their education and interests, were varied and elaborate and more sophisticated than mine. I was young but old enough to quickly appreciate that their way of life was much more attractive. They were all friendly and helpful, and the children formed deep attachments to them. I made friendships that summer which grew during my lifetime. I was awakened to the existence of a much more attractive side to life and determined that I would come back to camp at every opportunity. Buck seemed to enjoy his work tremendously, and it was fun living in his room with him, even though he did not spare me when it came to my share of doing whatever was necessary. Because he was head counselor, I was naturally on a more favorable relationship with most of the counselors; but he insisted that I go to bed at nine o'clock, the same time as the other children did.

When I entered high school after graduating from Brownell, I began to work at the C.E.A. at East 37 and Woodland as the page boy in the library. Even then I managed to spend a few weeks each summer as camp counselor. Those were the carefree, the fun loving, the happiest days I can remember; and many of the friendships we made there ripened during those teenage years into lifelong, precious comradeships.

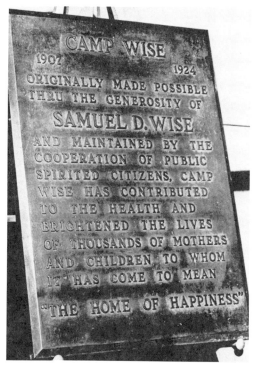

Tablet in Painesville camp memorializing Samuel D. Wise and the original Camp Wise near Euclid, Ohio, in Cuyahoga County. (H)

Another view of the mothers with babies quarters at the first Camp Wise, ca. 1918. (C)

Aerial view of Camp Wise second site, Painesville, Ohio, ca. 1926. (D)

The Home of Happiness, central building of Camp Wise, ca. 1930. (C)

Cleaning the tents in preparation for the next group of campers, ca. 1930. (D)

Jewish Orphan Home campers with boys' leader Al Brown, 1924. (C)

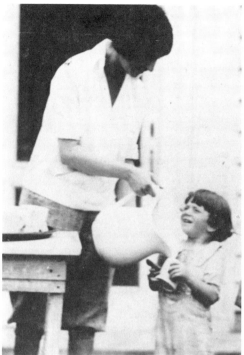 

All the milk you want. Irene Galvin pouring, 1924. (C)   Swimming costumes of the twenties, c. 1921. (C)

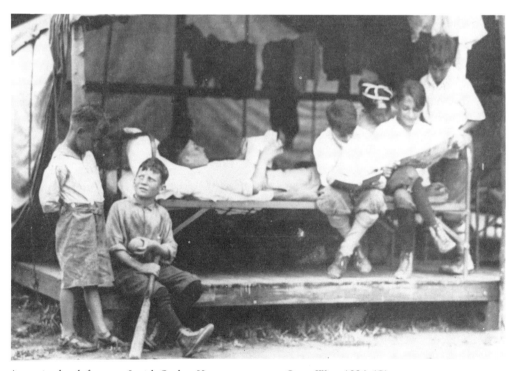

A vacation break for seven Jewish Orphan Home youngsters at Camp Wise, 1924. (C)

Girls getting ready for a hike to Nine-Mile Creek, 1924. (B)

The beach at Camp Wise after three days of rainstorms, 1924. (B)

If the girls can hike to Nine-Mile Creek, so can we. 1924. (C)

A group of mothers (and grandmothers, too) pose at Mothers' Camp section, 1933. (B)

The Camp Wise staff, 1934; among them, Matt Elson, who went on to national status in Jewish camping. (13)

An Alliwise camp reunion, 1927. (F)

Arabian Nites entertainment at camp by Alliwise members, 1954; Rose Mahrer, seated on floor, extreme right. (A)

Alliwise dance chorus, 1929. Left to right: William Levenson, Manny Lessem, Ruby Klein, Bernie Goldman, Charles Koch, Al Gilman, Irwin Dann, Manny Schreiben, Eli Rose, Henry Kutash; dancer instructor Sadie Siegel (Brown), center. (B)

A Camp Henry Baker contingent of boys and staff, 1937. First row seated, Matt Elson (6th from left), Manny Berlatsky (9th), and Abe Bonder (10th). (B)

Counselors and staff, Camp Wise, 1940; second row: Phil Wolfe (2nd from left), Spunk Kinoy (4th); third row: Ruth and Sidney Vincent (3rd and 4th). (B)

An afternoon marshmallow toast, 1942. Volunteers (left to right) Phyllis Kleinman, Cyril Schnit, Alice Rubin, Shirley Marks, Claire Alpern, and Rose Risk. (C)

Dorothy Wahl as Peep-Bo in a Camp Wise
performance of "The Mikado," 1932. (J)

Circus ringmasters Dave Hilberman, Jerry
Goldberg, and Joe Rosen in a camp performance,
ca. 1929. (J)

Its young builders named it Gypsy Camp, 1933. (J)

C.E.A. established its Camp Alliance next to Camp Wise in 1924, later renamed after benefactor Henry Baker, ca. 1930. (C)

A reunion of Camp Wise Crew members at their "Home of Happiness," ca. 1933. (J)

Camp Henry Baker girls, second trip, ca. 1940. In 1st row seated, Matt Elson (7th from left), Abe Bonder (9th), 1940. (B)

The U.S. Crop Corps of Camp Wise, farm labor on the home front, 1944. Leader Howard Robbins seated on the ground, center. (B)

War scrap drive at camp, ca. 1943-44. On the scrapheap Marilyn Weiss, William Leblang, and counselor Louis Chernikoff. (C)

Two dedicated Camp Wise-Alliwise stalwarts, Ida Schott and Dr. Leo Markey, 1948. (C)

Water fun in Lake Erie, ca. 1946. (C)

Honoring a friend, Hugo Mahrer, July 24, 1949. Left to right, Irwin Gold, Leon Weil, Myron Guren, Hugo Mahrer, George Hayes, and Harold Arian. (C)

The Camp Wise staff, 1958. Seated 6th from left, director Abe Bonder. (B)

Eager to start the hike, 1954. (C)

Counselors on the cliff training in the project method of camping, 1939. (C)

Camp Wise staff and counselors, 1942. First row seated: Lil Berkowitz (1st left), Harold Tannenbaum, director (4th), brothers Leonard and Richard Ronis (7th & 8th), Oscar Zimmerman (9th). (C)

Boy campers and their leaders, 1947. (B)

Girl campers and their leaders, 1947. (B)

Still another group of campers, 1958. (B)

Two notable figures in the Camp Wise story, Bill Treuhaft and "Uncle" Hugo Mahrer, July 24, 1949. (C)

Among the treasures to be found in the Cleveland Jewish Archives reposing at the Western Reserve Historical Society are three complete daybooks, or journals, carefully maintained by young leaders of Camp Wise over the summers of 1911, 1921, and 1923. Here we present excerpts from the earliest of those journals, exactly as they appear in the original typescript, fortuitous spellings, cavalier punctuation, and all. Emendations have been made only where a youthful finger had obviously struck a wrong key — the typewriter was, after all, a relatively newfangled device at the time.

The chroniclers of that 1911 daybook alternated daily from among a number of the volunteer leaders, but most of the following excerpts were written variously by Isadore ("Rube") Levy, Isadore Shane, Harry Rippner, B. ("Rip") Rippner, Sanford ("Sanny") Wiener, Reuben ("Rube") Levan, and David Rosenberg. They were all members of the UBY's (as explained earlier in this book, those letters are merely an alphabetic pun on "You Be Wise"), young men mostly from the German-Jewish establishment, who viewed their acceptance as volunteer leaders as a prestigious social plum and vied with one another for the opportunity to serve. The young women volunteers had no hand in this daybook but are referred to throughout its pages.

Unlike the regular full-time leaders, who stayed out at the camp for the entire period of their service, the UBY's were part-time volunteers, who worked at their jobs in the city during the day, then came out to camp in the evening, spent the night in their own tent just outside the camp proper, and returned early the next morning to the city. Weekends were spent entirely at camp. Another group of young volunteers, friendly competitors of the UBY's and also having their own tent, were the O'luvus, referred to frequently throughout this chronicle.

There are numerous references in the daybook entries to the horrors of rising at 5:30 A.M. in order to catch the 6:30 interurban into town. The main responsibility of the UBY's (although they made themselves useful in the kitchen or elsewhere as needed) was to entertain the campers in the evening with games, sports, plays, songs, stories, campfires, and the like; but as will be seen below, the week or weeks spent by the leaders at camp also offered them a splendid opportunity to socialize among themselves. At times, it seems, that was the chief motive for coming to camp. References in the daybook to the children campers themselves or to the mothers and babies are few and far between, almost never by name, and the snapshots scattered throughout the journal are mostly of the leaders.

The principal objective of the Council Educational Alliance and of the National Council of Jewish Women at that time was to Americanize the newly arrived immigrants and their children as quickly as possible, and that attitude is reflected in the camp journal. There is little in the entries even to suggest that this was a camp under Jewish auspices. The Sabbath was observed with the same activities as any other day. The songs taught and sung were all from the "American" tradition, and the few references to Yiddish, the mother tongue of most of the parents of the campers, are patronizing or contemptuous. On the other hand, German terms and expressions are sprinkled throughout. On a few occasions, a Rabbi Schwartz (presumably Rabbi Samuel Schwartz, who served the B'nai Jeshurun Congregation from 1909 to 1912) came out to camp, but apparently his only function was to tell (non-Jewish) stories to the campers. The head leader of the camp that year was Alex Warshawsky, usually referred to in the daybook by the shortened, Englished name "Warsaw."

The language in which the entries are written reflects the American slang of the period, including the deliberate misspellings ("laff" for laugh, "seegars" for cigars, "speshul" for special) that had been popularized by Artemus Ward and succeeding American humorous writers. Irony, often expressed by parenthesized question marks, is another comic device used throughout. As in the general community of those times, ethnic and racial pejoratives are used freely and unselfconsciously in a way that those with the greater sensitivity of our own times would find appalling.

But what chiefly characterizes this 1911 daybook of early Camp Wise is a joie de vivre, a camaraderie among these youthful leaders, and an innocence and optimism that belie the clouds of World War I just beyond the horizon.

David B. Guralnik

"It Has Been
A Glorious Summer. . . .":
The UBY's Log of 1911

Sunday, June 18, 1911

The season of 1911 for Camp UBY'S was formally opened today. Messrs. Shane, Levy and Rippner constituted the opening wedge and with two bottles of pickles, a hunk of bread, re-inforced with some Camp Wise coffee (?) we felt able to put up any old tent.

The building committee lined up as follows:

Mr. I. Levy - - - - - - - -BOSS.
Mr. H. Rippner - - - - - - Advisory Board.
Mr. Isodor Shane - - - - - The help.

Miss Moss kind of felt sorry for us and after we had the tent half up she kindly informed us that we would have to move. Many thanks Miss Moss. Of course had Miss Moss wanted to be real mean she could have waited until we had the tent entirely finished. We all danced with joy upon hearing this news, Rube in particular could scarcely contain himself, he was so tickled.

We moved next to our friends, the enemy Camp O'luvus, they are all Hibernians, as the name indicates, and means in our language 'I love my chicken but oh you Camp Wise Mush and Milk'.

After *purchasing* some new beams and flooring we proceeded with our work. Under Mr. Levy's capable direction the work fast neared completion and by six P.M. we had three beams and a cross-piece ready, so we knocked off work for the day.

Went to Willow Beach for supper (Rube had some friends there, with basket lunches) and after eating a hearty meal we came back to camp. Mr. Levy was called away by business, and Messrs. Rippner and Shane remained to hold down above mentioned beams and cross-pieces.

It was a beautiful, dreamy, moonlit night so we went to sleep early.

P.S. We *purchased* some more flooring before turning in.

Monday, June 19th, 1911

Shane and Rippner finished up the flooring and hoisted the tent, with the capable assistance of Mr. B. Rippner. Of course we don't want to brag because the work is a mere bag of shells, ask Rube.

All the Kids and LEADERS came out today and things began to assume their normal Camp Wise appearance. . . .

I found out something today: Shane smokes stogies, also, there is a nifty little bakery wagon comes around every day about noon, also there are cherries on the road to Noble.

Mr. L. Fried, our eminent SOCIALIST friend from next door expounded the doctrine of brotherly love and universal helpfulness to us all day but he was so busy talking that the bugger did not give us a lift all day. P.S. I am going to turn Socialist, it's a damfine thing.

Turned in very early after a very strenuous and fatigueing day.

Tuesday, June 20, 1911

Up at 6:30 this morning for our breakfast. Got up early upon the advice of Mr. Shane, as he said that we would get more to eat. We did —not. Just the same, mush and lots of it tasted pretty fine.

We each got a squad — Oh how we love our squads. You start out with five boys, five brooms and one prayer, answer about five million foolish questions, tell each boy just what to do and then end up by doing most of the work yourself. . . .

In passing, Camp UBY'S is now carpeted with a nifty nile green and in spots dirty yellow burlap (the spots are where Shane stepped) Visitors please take note. The only possible objection is that the color is not fast and the soles of our feet are all colored a beautiful green.

This organ is not in the habit of throwing boquets, but we must say that our Leaders of the present week are the nicest, best looking, most genial, pleasantest and most attractive that we have seen out here————this year.

Wednesday, June 21, 1911

The two R's — Rube and Rip, went in for a duck this morning — Believe me when Rube gets up early enuf in the morning to be able to take a swim — it's deserving of mention. Rube just about backed out at the last minute at that — it was too c-c-cold for him.

There was a dance on tap at the hotel tonight and we certainly had some fine time. Mr. Hi Firman our terpsichorean expert, glid around very graceful all evening and gave a little tone to the affair, by his prescence (He certingly is the accomadating old scout). Sanny [Wiener] slid in after the affair was well under way but once there, he more than made up for lost time, Sanny is getting to be some Kid. . . .

Thursday, June 22, 1911

Ha- I knew that mush would give out some time, we had wheat biscuits for breakfast. Maybe after all that is'nt it — I guess it's easier to serve wheat biscuits. . . .

Mr. B. Rippner, disregarding our advice played ball in the sun in a gym shirt today — Result; —Mr. Rippner will sleep on his stomach for a few days to come and will thank all his friends to *bust* away from his shoulders.

Mr. Shane is trying hard to cultivate a dark tan — for why, easy; then he will never have to wash. . . .

It is a beautiful night, the stars shining high above give a mingled sence of serenity and security. The moon rides high in the heavens and shining down upon us gives promise of better things. Ah — On such a night as this —Holy gee it's getting late and Shane is snoring already.

Saturday, June 24, 1911

One big day — got up early — for our "Mushandmilk" Played ball — Kids went for a hike and had a general grand time all day. . .

Messrs. Levy and Rippner brought back some Asaphaetedi [asafetida] (which sounds fine but smells like hell) and rubbed about a ton of it in Mr. Shane's pillow. Mr. Shane lies down, gently murmurs, "who opened the bottle of Cologne" and drops into a profound if not noiseless slumber. That's the trouble with that sucker, we spend a nickel for dope, nearly break a leg getting things all fixed up for him, and then he can't tell the difference between a rose bush and a limburger cheese sandwitch. . . .

Sunday, June 25, 1911

Altho the previous night had been a strenuous one we were all on the job for breakfast early this morning. Raining and things looked rather bad. It cleared up tho and by ten o'clock everything was dry and ship shape. . . .

Played the boys next door in the afternoon —the UBY'S boys of course starred. Mr. Shane made the prize bone head play of the afternoon on first base, Mr. Levy however made up for him by a magnificent exhibition of UMPIRING

— if it had not been for several wonderful plays by Rube — we surely would have lost. Mr. H. Rippner's work was of course easily the feature of the game. The less said about it the better. Old FAT High Firman of the O'luvus wobbled around in right field. We only mention him in passing as of course he had no real part in the game. . . .

Monday, June 26, 1911

. . . A new set of Leaders out this week and who do you suppose are amongst them? Nunst other than the the the two sin twisters Cora & Sadie [Lederer]. They may be small but 'oh my; I wonder if there is anything serious between Shane and one of those girls?. . . .

A COMPARISON

Mr. Sanford Wiener our pride and boast, rolled in about ten P.M. lit his flash light, took off his coat, hung it carefully on a hanger, removed his shoes and socks, placed them were he could get at them without trouble in the morning, divested himself of the rest of his garments, rubbed witch hazel on his pitching arm, manicured his nails, put on his pan-jamas, wound up his watch, shook out his pillow and then retired calmly into a deep noiseless slumber.

Mr. Brute Shane, busts in the tent about eleven o'clock smashes his head against the oil lamp, stubs his toe on the flooring, swears loud enough to wake the dead, pain-stakingly goes from bed to bed in the dark and wakes everybody up. This done to his entire satisfaction he throws his sweater (I beg your pardon, I should have said Rip's sweater) under his bed, kicks his shoes (they are his) in the next tent, throws the rest of his duds right and left, takes a flying leap into the debris, that is supposed to represent his bed. Stretches his legs over into Rip's bed and inside of two minutes, the concert is on. . . .

The following is a contribution of the editor's at which we trust no one will take offense, it is meant well:

> There was a young feller named Is
> Who had such a comical Phyz
> That he lay himself down
> Turned a nifty dark brown
> Now nobody knows who Is is.

> There is amongst us out here,
> One who need never know fear
> With his medicine chest
> And his eight hour rest
> Sam Wiener is with us this year.

There is a young feller called Rube
Who used to be fed thro a tube
But he ate such a lot
That they called it all rot
Now Is feeds with his hands like a boob.

Lots of fun, and we turned in rather late with the thoughts of a hearty meal of MUSHAND before us. . . .

Tuesday, June 27, 1911

. . . Awful storm today, about noon — Shane who was taking care of the tent was eating at the time; natural consequence was that the fly blew down and all of our bedding got soaked thro and thro. Mr. Shane finished his repast some thirty minutes later, leisurely strolls out, and wonders "how come" that the tent is down. Note — Mr. Shane's bed was inside the tent, while all the rest of the boy's stuff was out in the fly. No gentle reader, Mr. Shane's bedding did not get wet. . . .

Up to the hotel and played KEENO. Rube nearly won a kiss, He got a couple later tho, from the cook. Sat on the porch then and had lots of fun, reading the diary.

Miss Moss entertained with stories of "her Children." Mr. Levan and Miss S. Lederer gave an exhibition of their railroad laugh. What a beautiful duet they do give. Sadie laughs horrible to Rube's "rotten". . . .

We were then invited over to Camp O'luvus to help break in their visitor. Believe me they broke him in. Mr. Hirsch, is his name and we certainly showed him some fine time. This is the way it goes; — First you sit around and eat a lot of hard nuts and throw the shells in the victims bed (where he is already sleeping) then get some good, stout cord and tie him firmly, but gently in his bed, then some one turns out the light and some heavy object; preferably an iron rail, however a shoe is a good substitute; is brought down on the victims head, and then the bed is dumped over. Everybody hides, and the victim of course laughs gently and inquires after everybody's health and then goes back to bed —with a club and two shoes in each hand. . . .

Thursday, June 29th, 1911

When we left the camp this morning Mr. Shane was still sleeping — he was up too late the night before. I know her name but I'm not going to tell. Oh yes, he got up in time to get some breakfast all right. . . .

Sat around after the Kids went to bed, and watched Shane and his friend, cut up. For a girl her size, C— certainly is a terror with the boys. I tremble to think of how she will behave when she grows up. Miss S.L. absolutely refuses to laff any more, says she is insulted on account of the notoriety we gave her in a previous issue. Aw come on Kid, don't be tight, we like it and besides laughing makes you fat. Look at Rube.

Mr. Fried our Socialist friend was laid up with a severe ache. Must have swallowed some of his own talk. . . .

PLAYLET

TITLE   —   Wake Me Early Mother Dear, Wake Me Early.
TIME   —   Any old morning.
PLACE   —   Camp Wise on the Lake.

Scene: — Front fly of Camp UBY'S.
In the foreground is seen two cots, with two heads and two pairs of feet sticking out of each end. Hi Firman is gently rubbing his cold, clammy hands on the small of Rube's back to arouse him, which he finally succeeds in doing.

Act. I. Scene I.

Rube   R-r-rip, g-g-goin' in s-s-swimmun'
Rip   Aw shut up don't bother me.

Silence — and lots of it.

Ten minutes later Rip wakes up.

Rip   Hey Rube, get up if you'r goin' in the water.
Rube   Aw not now, lets sleep awhile yet.
Rip   Come on, now or never
Rube   (Sticks his head out from the blankets) Ur-r-r-r its t-t-too c-c-cold.
Rip   Climb a tack then, I'll go alone.
Rube   Aw be a sport Rip, let's sleep ten minutes more then we'll
           both go in.
Rip   Think it's about four o'clock, I suppose
Rube   Five minutes then
Rip   Nope
Rube   Two minutes.
Rip   Nothun' doin.
Rube   Till I count Five.
Rip   Answers by pulling all the covers off Mr. Rube.
Rube   (In the back tent) H-h-holy smokers those r-r-r-rotten t-t-tights are
           w-w-wet, wh-where that-t-t-t st-t-tiff Shane. St-t-talls around all
           d-d-day and hasn't even g-g-got time to dry our b-b-b-bathing
           suit-t-ts. Ur-r-r its c-c-cold.
Rip   Hey mut — aint you ready yet.

Rube   G'wan in yourself if y-y-youre s-s-so nutt-tty about it-t-t. I'm g-g-going b-b-back t-t-to b-b-bed. B'r-r-r-r it's c-c-cold.

CURTAIN

Friday, June 30, 1911

. . . Nothing much on tap tonight so we had to hang around the tent and start an argument. Hi Firman carried off the honors: that geek can tell lies with such a straight face that there aint any come back. Then we started off to Noble for some oil for our lamp and for some provisions (Honest Scrap and Tuxedo [pipe tobacco] for Shane) We got as far as the kitchen and there the milk and "Kuchen" proved too much of a temptation, so we didn't get any farther.

While sitting on the porch at about 9 P.M. we heard the Buffalo boat tooting and blazing like all possessed and throwing its Searchlight over the shore and across the waters. Of course we all immediately concluded that the boat was in distress and ran down to the shore with dreadful visions of sudden death and tragedy before our eyes. Miss Moss hailed the boat, but somehow or other they did not seem to hear and there we were utterly helpless to help the poor doomed souls on board the vessel. It soitenly was turrible. Slowly and with scarcely a perceptible motion the ship moved on, and like a monster of the deep, cruelly wounded, she at last faded from our sight. Wondering and speculating we crept to our seats utterly despondent, yet unable to give even a helping hand. Oh cruel, cruel Fate. We found out the next day that all this fuss that the boat had made namely the horn blowing and the throwing of the searchlight, was for the special benefit of Miss Irene Hirscheimer. Gee there's another good mystery exploded. . . .

Before closing: a word about the LEADERS of the present week. We have perhaps before given praise to other Leaders but we have never before, met so industrious, so reserved, so painstaking, so sweet and all the things we called the other Leaders last week, a set of Young Ladies and Men, as those who are this week carrying the responsibilities and difficulties of this institution on their shoulders. Note: This part is not for Leaders. Of course this is all bunko, but they seem to expect it and it fills up space, and so as Toblitsky says; — "Vy not". . . .

Sunday, July 2nd, 1911

. . . About 11 o'clock the visitors started pouring in and we watched them very carefully — we kept our eyes especially on the basket lunches. Later when the visitors were engrossed in some other pleasant pursuit we *purchased* oranges, bananas and sandwitches.

Ball game after dinner and as usuall we skunk the visitors, They never even had a chance. We ran around the bases so long and often that we lost track of the score. Mr. Hi Firman played a star game — on the bench. Little Mr.

Neumark it seems has a sore finger — anyway everytime he misses a ball he shoves that finger in his mouth and makes contortions denoting dreadful agony. Poor boy. I feel sorry for him. So do we all. Mr. Alex Warsaw, he of the bum shoulders and glass arm played a bang up game at short. Lev umpired, Brut played first, and Mr. Harry A. Rippner caught. . .

Monday, July 3rd, 1911

. . . Sad news — Camp Wise got licked in a base ball game today by the Goodrich boys. Whats the matter Alex — didn't they give you a chance to call the game when our boys were ahead? . . .

Miss Ida Schott is one of the Leaders this week. Miss Schott like wine improves every year. We mean this too, as we have no particular reason to boost Miss S. She was our teacher in our youthful days and we still have a rather vivid remembrance of a piece of glue and paper which was pasted over our mouth. Also Miss S. was the reason for several whalings which we received. . . .

Tuesday, Fourth of July, 1911

Mr. Ben Dietz, one of our industrious workers about the grounds, started shooting off a young cannon about Five A.M. and of course woke everybody up.

We forgot to report that some few days ago, Saturday to be exact. Two of our Real Bright Young Men, Mr. Rippner accompanied by Mr. Levy swiped two perfectly good bycicles from the grounds and went out for a little joy ride. Fifteen minutes later could be seen above mentioned Bright Young Men, trudging back to Camp along the road from Willow Beach; heaving a very sadly bent and twisted bycicle on their shoulders. It cost fore said R.B.Y.M. exactly Two Fifty, to make things right and now are very much sadder and wiser MEN.

We went boating with our friends and O'luvus and you can take it from me we had some fine time. Rowed out about two miles and Mr. Jack Stacel swam the entire distance in to shore. Mr. Rippner also followed part way — hanging on to the hind end of the boat. When nearing shore a very disastrous and almost fatal mishap occured. Somehow or other the boat tipped to far to one side and in another moment we were all struggling for our lives in the water. We surely would have drowned only for the presence of mind of Mr. Levan. He kept his head and told us to walk ashore, which we did. Mr. Blum lost One pair tennis slippers, one pair perfectly good socks, one pair hose supporters, and his trousers and raincoat were beautifully soaked. He claims a loss of $3.75. We took up a collection of course and gave this amount to Little Jeff — did'nt we fellows (all together now) Yes we did — NOT. Any how we had a glorious time and in the process Rube had his knees and toes sunburnt. . . .

Overheard at the fire work display in the evening. Mr. Isodor Grossman chasing a little girl back from the firing line says I suppose you want to get all black and have two or three of your eyes burnt and six or seven feet scorched.

Immediately after supper the annual fire work display was started. Mr.

Clay Baker sent up a few balloons with good success. The only trouble with some of those balloons was that they were so full of holes that they wouldnt fly, otherwise they were perfectly all right. Then the real display was on. Red lights, green lights sky rockets, roman candles, flower pots and all the rest of the FOURTH OF JULY paraphanalia was there and maybe the Kids didn't have the time of their young lives. Ice Cream was served and after that they were chased to bed. . . .

Wednesday, July 5th, 1911

. . . 'Twas so warm today that we ate picnic lunches out on the grass tonight. The ant sandwitches were vera good. Mr. Hi Firman discoursed on the selfishness of some of the boys — It seems that those who are first at the table load up on the grub and those who come in later are stuck. Hi has been late at the table for the past few nights, that's the reason for this change of heart. Cheer up Kid — Shane is not going to take his supper here anymore: so we will all have a chance now. . . .

Jokes on Rube — Mr. Reuben lying on the grass on a certain young ladie's (Who's name we shall not mention) lap; takes the young ladies hand and caresses it fondly — holds said hand to his lips makes an awful fuss generally over it — You know — Looks at the hand a little more closely and following the hand up finds Hi Firman at the other end of it. We near died laffin. . . .

Thursday, July 6th, 1911

. . . Amateur night at the hotel; and the programme was not exactly what one would call brilliant but it wasn't so rotten either. Miss Sonia Auerbach a little german girl with a "sauerkraut and wiener" accent sticking out from all four sides of her carried off the honors. Mr. Sol Maretsky gave a violin solo and it certainly was a great exhibition — of nerve. After a long and heated argument amongst the Leaders it was finally decided to give him the prize.

WHOS WHO AND WHY

Whenever the dishes look extra clean and the spoons a little brighter than usual its a cinch that the Leader twins, Cora and Sadie [Lederer] are out.

They don't care much what we have to eat, or whether the floor is clean or not, their specialty is dishes and believe me those dishes get theirs when they are bossing the job. Why we noticed one poor dish that lost two pounds in one week while the girls were here.

Cora and Sadie are not exactly twins but they jibe together so nicely that you can't help but call them so, For instance, Cora sings soprano and Sadie tenor — Cora is younger but Sadie is handsomer — Cora wears number nine shoes and Sadie Number tens. Well when you think of all that why then if they ain't twins they ought to be.

One of the best things the girls do is to laff and such a nice pleasant laff as they have got — like a steam caliope. They will laff at anything from Piggy Blum to a rainy day.

The girls are both vera, vera clever and just as sweet as can be. The best thing about Cora is Is Shane and the best thing about Sadie is Cora...

Both girls are old stand byes out to the Camp and they like the Camp and the Camp likes them better every year. Both are school ma'arms but after you know them for about two minutes you won't hold that against them.

As they say in the classics they are small but — Oh my They are awful funny sisters in a way. They act like perfect strangers - never fight, think a whole lots of each other and are not afraid to say so. Any one who didn't know'em never suspect that they were sisters. . . .

Friday, July 7th, 1911

Today was a rather quiet day out to the camp and nothing very funny or interesting was pulled off. (If the truth were told the editor is writing this up on Monday July 10th. and it's pretty hard remembering all the foolish things that happened so long ago). . . .

Saturday, July 8th, 1911

Rube and Rip had a day off today — so we slept late, We had Sanny wake us early so we could tell him to go to work and laff at him. We ate with the Kids and as a reward for oversleeping we had an extra good meal — Mush and Sour Milk. . . .

Went to Euclid Beach in the afternoon, where Rip participated in a ball game. Rube also played BAWL: he Bawled out Rip and his team every chance he got. Rube is what you call an optimist. The only thing he never finds fault with is himself. . ..

Mr. Leo Neumark arrived today — He said that the girls sent for him. Ain't Leo the little heart breaker tho? . . .

This is a song dedicated to the Farewell of Miss Babby Moss. It has been written co-jointly by Miss Sadie Lederer and Mr. Harry Rippner. It is sung to the tune of "Just One Camp" our old familiar Camp Wise song. The writers appreciate that the rhythm may be rotten, we know that there are too many feet in some lines, we feel that some of the words are mis-pelled but we are dead sure and we are positive that all of our readers will agree with us that the sentiments are right.

TO BABBY MOSS

There is out here
A leader dear

Who soon from us must part.
She loves us all
Both great and small
To leave will break her heart.

Her children fair
Will miss her care
And long to see her face
She may be gone
But not for long
For none can take her place

So now 'twill be
Farewell to thee
Our dear beloved boss
Till you return
For you will yearn
Goodbye Miss Babby Moss.

CHORUS

Just one Babby
And she's the one we sing to
Just one Babby
The only girl for us

Sunday, July 9th, 1911

Mr. Reuben Levan in his artless way had swiped four of "Humphries Best" pop corn balls the previous night so of course he had to wake us all up at an unearthly hour and we filled ourselves and the beds with pop corn. . . .

Rube, Rip and Shane strung up about a dozen and a half mirrors for Miss Bernstein. Sunday's our day of rest you know. . . .

Played ball in the afternoon and we had one fine game. Batteries for Camp Wise — Jeff and Mutt (Rip And Sanny) Beat the opposition to the tune of Twenty to Three and had a regular walkaway. Mr. Jay Halle, he of the long flowing mane and Jimjeffry shoulders was the batting hero. Jay got a triple and two doubles, the last time that Jay got a hit in a real ball game Mayor McKisson, declared a legal holiday.

The right honorable Doc. Mr. Grossman umpired and did a very good job of it too. Doc certainly had the other fellows scared stiff. . . . Mr. Leo Neumark was the bright shining star — he nearly won the game — for the other fellows. Solid Ivory, Kiddo. At that he played a nice game.

After the game we went for a little row. We did not intend to take Mr.

Levy with us but after he had turned the boat over and thrown us in the water, we thought better of it. We rowed down to Miss Moss at stop 136-1/2 and believe me that's some little row. . . We finally got there and after a pleasant little walk in our bare feet [on] a cinder path — we arrove. We were treated to some whisky (Doc said it was alright as a stimulant) and had a hard job breaking away. . . .

Tuesday, July 11th, 1911

. . . Marshmellow roast down at the lake front tonight. How those Kids can get on the outside of marshmellows. Sample: "Mr. Grossman give me a marshmellow, I ain't got none yet" at the same time wiping his sticky hands on the side of his trousers. . . .

Overheard on the campus: ball game in progress: "Abie KNOCK the ball to first". . . .

Wednesday, July 12th, 1911

Tonight was a big night: the dance at the hotel, and to state that it was a success is to put it mildly. The whole surrounding country side was there including most of the Goodrich Camp and visitors from Cleveland and the affair was run off with the utmost eclat. Messrs. Stacel and Doc Grossman composed the orchestra and they certainly earned their money. There is one feature of Doc's dances that ain't always so nice; the Good Lord help you if you ever get a punk partner, for those dances last at the very least a half an hour. Mr. Rippner was unusually honored; a young lady asked him for the next dance. You see that's what it means to be big and handsome. N.B. Mr. R. neglected to state that the young lady was about two foot high and could just about talk. Mr. Shane felt slightly indisposed and did not dance. After dancing our heads off the affair wound up with a grand march which was run off to the beautiful inspiring strains of THE STAR SPANGLED BANNER. Then that grandest of all songs "GOOD NIGHT LADIES" was sung and the Kids were in bed. . . .

Returned and joined the crowd down at the point. Arrived in time to hear Rabbi Schwartz finish up a cute little fairy tale. It was very good and we laid around in a bunch like a page out of the Arabian Nights. If you ever want to see how little room a bunch of people really need, come down there some time. After the doctor was finished we had some funny stories and experiences, from others in the crowd. Irene Hirscheimer was present and told some stories to a few that made an instantaneous hit. . . .

Thursday, July 13th, 1911

. . . Big doings tonight — Amateur night and a very big audience. Mr. Jay Halle was stage manager and general announcer and he did a good job, except once or twice when he got his signals crossed and announced a solo when as a matter of fact a recitation was up. Somebody was heard to remark that the Amateur Night performances were good things for the children as it tended to give them confidence in themselves. Ye Gods — Do those Kids need any more confidence. If brass was gold each one of our stars would be a mint. Taken as a whole the performance was very good and was thoroly enjoyed. Talk about your variated bill — we had songs in English, German and Yiddish, recitations in English, German and Baby Talk, Jokes, violin solo and a pony ballet. The Pony Ballet was one of the big features of the entertainment. Drilled by Miss Clarice Mittleberger — eight boys and girls gave an excellent rendition of Jimmy Valentine. The scenic effects were truly wonderful, they consisted of a pocket flash, and lots of darkness. Miss Mittleberger then went on with THE act of the evening, and scored a tremendous success with several songs and dances. Gertrude Hoffman had better look to her laurels. To top it off the Kids lined up and each one received a pop corn ball, the gift of Mr. Wise, and then ended a wildly, exhilarating evening by giving three cheers for Mr. Wise. . . .

Sunday, July 16th, 1911

We arose with the larks — 7:30 A.M. and we had to hustle to get in for breakfast. Some way or other we always manage to get there in time for breakfast —we might be shy a collar or one or two shoes or perhaps a shirt — but we get there and thats the main thing.

Being as its Sunday, a little cleaning up was in order and we fixed up the beds in fine style. Gave all the sheets and pillow slips a French Bath (turned them on the other side) and slicked up generally. Rube kicked said it was too early in the season for that — he will have to bring out a new pillow case before the season is over. At that when one of our fair visitors saw his pillow slip later in the day — she suggested turning it over so as to have the clean side uppermost. . . .

Doc Wiener — hereafter if you please. Sanny fixed up three or four awful gashes on Mr. Rippner's feet in great style. He handles his medical outfits like a professional — ditch digger. After he gets thro mauling you up he solicitiously inquires "Did it hurt" Oh No" Whatinell's the use of hollerin' after its all over. . . .

Altho it poured steadily all afternoon we had a big bunch of visitors. They amused themselves by reading this log and looking at Rube. Later we had dancing. The visitors all had lunches, but wanted them for themselves. My what a tight bunch. . . .

Monday, July 17th, 1911

This was some morning — a blinding flash of lightning that seemed to tear the whole tent from end to end woke us up about 3 o'clock and we found that the rain was coming down in torrents. Lots of excitement until we got our beds in out of the rain. We finally fell asleep, but it was still pouring great guns when we got up. We managed to wade thro the campus for breakfast and had to eat in the main room as our room was full of water. We all got most thoroly and artistically soaked goin for the car. . . .

Stayed in the hotel tonight as it was a raw cold night. Had a little dance which we wound up, with one of our old fashioned, hilarious Virginia Reels, Doc Grossman played for us and you can believe we had some fun. We clapped our hands, stamped our feet, grand right and lefted, and Do Se Doed until we were almost ready to drop. Mr. Geismer led the Reel and was chief instructor. Thats good lung exercise Mr. Geismer. . . .

Tuesday, July 18th, 1911

. . . We had a marshmellow roast for the Kids down by the cliff, and we toasted marshmellows and also toasted our faces. Mr. Geismer led in our Camp Wise song, which also passed a pleasant hour or so. We then send the Kids to Bed

Promptly upon the dissapearance of the youngsters the Camp Wise Kaffe-Klatsch was called to order on the porch and we had a general discussion Mr. Alex Warsaw doped out the days ball game for us and tried to figure out how the Naps scored nine runs in one inning. Al got as far as "Larry singled and the crowd went wild" and then had to give it up. Concentration Al, Concentration.

Miss Schwartz had an interesting argument with herself on the latest book that she has read. It deals with the philosophy of Theoretical Altruism. thats why she had to argue with herself. Dost know what it means gentle reader, darned if I do. . . .

Wednesday, July 19th, 1911

Looked like it might turn out to be a nice day, when we got up. Mr. "Carl Marx" Fried came in to breakfast, late. Fried swears up and down every night before retiring that he won't eat the next day, as its healthy to fast occasionally. But he always turns up the last minute and then bawls the other fellows out for eating his share. . . .

Tonight was "DANCE NIGHT" and we had a goodly crowd. As a special added attraction we had some terpsichorean numbers by some of our small visitors. We sprinkled wax (which we had purchased) On the floor, making it as smooth and slippery as glass. (That might not be absolutely true but it sounds well) Numerous youngsters made their debut on the floor tonight, and found the going rather rough on account of the glassy floor. Miss Oppenheim was in great demand by the Kids. Gee, I wish I was a good dancer. . . .

Thursday, July 20th, 1911

. . . Leo Neumark was out tonight and we got him to give us a full detailed account of the ball game, of which we had of course read a full detailed account shortly before. Talk about your shining marks. Leo, you get a hundred. Yes Leo brought a young lady along with him. Clarice Mittleberger was also here tonight and sort o' made it feel like old times. . . .

The Leaders left for the point about ten o'clock and we left for the hay. We fixed up Manny Barkin's bed for him very artistically, decorating it with old shoes, baseball bats, iron spikes, wash dishes, wet paper, and other sundries. We took especial pains to hide the lamp and all the matches, and then Mr. Manny strolls in about 12:30 and calmly lights up his flash light and of course gets wise. Darn those things anyway, Anyhow I ain't got any use for a guy that will look in his bed before turning in. Mr. Barkin distributed his gifts impartially to all the boys and then with a clear conscience and a whole hide went to sleep.

Friday, July 21st, 1911

Lovely day — no excitement during the day — once in a while we have those kind of days out here. . . .

After supper the youngsters played cowboys and Indians — both sides claimed victory. "Pewee" Blum played and fell asleep while hiding: the fellows wanted to ditch him, but thought better of it because when Doc Grossman, Jack Steele, Miss Schwartz, Charley Dietz and four or five others ain't around we have to depend on Pewee for our music. . . .

Plutocrat Blum and Common People Fried had a heated argument on why it is that I have money and you haven't. Plute sort o' hung it on old C.P. Fried. . . .

Glorious night and we sat on the porch till 10:30, and then turned in. The Leaders went down to the point and from the waves of laffter which reached us from there, we inferred that they were having a good time. Mr. Rosenberg wanted to resign his job as keeper of the light but after much argument in three languages (English, Sane and Profane) he saw the error of his ways, and turned out the glim.

Saturday, July 22nd, 1911

. . . Mr. Sanford Wiener our millionare member went to work this morning for the first time in two weeks — at that its only for one little morning. Pretty soft for some guys. San had to get rid of some of his mileage tickets, so he sold us fifteen cents of car ride for thirteen cents, We know at least one man who on the strength of that two cents saving spent ten cents on cigars.

The editor came out at about two P.M. and had a peculiar experience. While waiting for the car at 105th Street a car came by with another one about two blocks behind. Our old friend Stein was conducting the first car and when we asked him if the second car went all the way thro, he up and says "yes" So we waited for the second car in order to get a seat. The second car went thro all right, but without the Right Honorable Mr. Editor. 'Twas an Electric Package. . . .

Sunday, July 23rd, 1911

. . . Rip, Rube, and Sanny went over to Oakwood Club in the afternoon to play against that team and went over in an AUTO. See what it means to be good ball players. We had one fine ride only the tire blew out a half a mile from our destination and we had to walk until another auto picked us up. We lost the game but had another fine auto ride home, which sorto' made up. . . .

Wednesday, July 26th, 1911

. . . Heard at the fire the other night — Some one said "Thank you Kindly" in German and Shane wanted to know who was talking to him. "Thank you kindly" in German goes like this "Donkey Shane".

When the boys came out tonight our tent was a sight — all the beds were overturned and our bedding and clothing piled in a disreputable heap in the back of the tent. This tickled us immensely and we had a regular picnic cleaning up. Sure —you know thats what we like — do a hard days work in town and then come in to camp and put in another or two hours work. . . .

We neglected to mention in our yesterday issue — that Mr. Isadore Levan alias "Rube" celebrated his 21st birthday. Rube's a man and will vote the straight Republican ticket. From now on Rube will dress himself and it will no longer be necessary to tuck him in bed at night. Hats off to the New Citizen of the United States of America. . . .

Our new Camp Wise National Antherm — "Will you Marry - Me - Me - Me -Doc plays it as a waltz, two step schottiche or Cuban Waltz — some class to Doc.

Mr. Davy Rosenberg went into the Kitchen for water tonight and got it — from a cup., Judiciously placed on the top of the kitchen door.

Miss Freeman & Wachs mysteriously disappeared about 8:30 and did not show up till late — we turned in about 10:30 but they were still missing at that time. Carefull Miss F. don't teach Walt any bad habits.

> The night was cold and chilly,
> The clouds rolled on high.
> The lightning flashed in vivid streaks,
> Athwart a darkened sky.
>
> B-r-r-r- Good Night.

Friday, July 28th, 1911

Quiet day today — nothing much doing. At night the youngsters played around on the grass and listened to stories.

Two distinguished members of Camp O'luvus put up a great joke on their high browed friend Walter Wachs. When Walt went to turn in — he first of all found a big, fat deceased owl staring him in the face. Walt promptly threw a fit and after stabbing the dead fowl he grabbed it by ten foot or more of string and chased madly to the shore with it. He returned and announced that we could all go to sleep as he had killed the chicken. Climbing in bed Mr. Wachs encountered two more of the same kind and talk about scared. The best Walter could do for five minutes or so was to stutter. Note; he also said "dam" Walter ain't exactly what you would call a hero and after these awful experiences he could hardly get up enuff nerve to go to bed.

Went up to the porch where we were regaled with a hearty meal consisting of pop corn, taffy and peanuts, which were brought out by Marc Grossman. You see Marc was out here for over a week and he has a fellow feeling for us. From there we went down to the beach and sat around and had a fine time. . . .

Saturday, July 29th, 1911

. . . Went down to the point later and had a rather nice albeit quiet time. Camp O'luvus was also there and of course they had a high browed discussion on some light subject (I guess 'twas the immortality of the soul) Joe Denby gave his views and of course that settles it for all time. Gee that's a funny bunch — they see a rock on the ground and immediately thats cause for a long and serious controversy.

One of them will say — Say boys just think how old that rock is.

Next One	I'll bet its lain here thousands of years.
Next One	I wonder how it come here.
Answer	I think its a part of a metoer
Question	What's a metoer?
Answer	Part of planet
Somebody else	No its a constellation

There you are — inside of two minutes the whole gang will be arguing and fighting over the "Nebulous theory of the earth's foundation" and the chances are that by 11:30 that night it will be veered around to Race Suicide. The original cause of the argument — was probably thrown by a kid at a stray dog, that day — Great crowd that. . . .

Sunday, July 30th, 1911

. . . Had a fine dinner and the way we dived into the watermelon was a caution. If you want to get a line on a fellow's make up — watch him eat watermelon. For instance San Wiener places his piece carefully on a clean plate, gently picks up his knife and fork, cuts off a dainty piece, looks it over on all sides and then places it carefully in his mouth being very sure that he chews it seventy two times before swallowing. Mr. Levy grabs a great big piece of melon off the tray, before it is even laid down. puts both his elbows on the table, loosens his collar and then jams his face up to the ears in the melon. Lifts his head, wipes the juice out of his eyes and then repeats the performance. Most of the fellows are just starting on their second mouthful when Rube grabs his plate and hustles in the kitchen for another hunk. . . .

Our Leaders of this week leave tonight and it is with regret we see them go. Fearless in their duty, consciencious in their work, strong in their faith, and all the rest of that — they have won our undying admiration and appreciation. Goodby folks and come again.

The Banqueters:

Mr. Sanford Wiener   *Toastmaster*
Mr. David Rosenberg   *An Eater*
Mr. Isadore Shane   *An Eater Extraordinary*
Mr. Harry Rippner   *An Eater — also not so rotten*
Mr. Isadore Levy   *Our Toast "My Brod"*

Some of the toasts:

Here's to our Rube — May his day be as long as his jokes.
If he doesn't die in the *gallows* its a nickel to nothing he chokes?

Legs and Freckles — Skin and Bone
Red hair — big feet — lazy drone.
Laffs and giggles like a boob
Still we like him — 'Rah for Rube.

Monday, July 31st, 1911

. . . We hired a new man to take care of our tent. We pay him the munificent sum of five cents per day — what do we care for expences. . . .

Tuesday, August 1st, 1911

We have been repeatedly questioned on the editorial policy of this paper and to settle this question we will say that our motto is:

"Hew to the line — let the chips fall where they may"

Our beloved and popular editor went to work this morning, turned around and came right back again. Those midnight lunches got in their deadly work and put even his cast iron stomach on the blink. Dear friends: Didst ever know what is perfect bliss? Ride for one hour and five minutes on a stuffy bucking rip snorting suburban car with a severe case of indigestion. Believe us the solid, steady ground will look like "The Happy Hunting Grounds" and oh how you would like to get off and walk only you're to weak to ring the bell.

Mr. Ralph Sloss constituted himself head nurse and fed the patient "Paregoric" he said it was two table spoons full every two hours — We know better however it was a dipperfull every ten minutes. Mr. Sam Rosenberg sat alongside and told of all the people that he had known to die of similar attacks —you know to kind of cheer the patient up. In spite of their combined efforts Mr. Rippner was ready for Miss Sloss convalescent lunch at 5:00 P.M. Believe me that lunch more than made up for everything. . . .

Our electric light was not working tonight and we had to go to the old primitive lamp and candle light. We have dim recollections that yah and yeahs ago, we had to depend on such light. . . .

Friday, August 4th, 1911

Nice day — Kids went out for a hike today and from all accounts it was a complete success. . . .

We had visitors tonight. Miss Martha Markowitz and a friend. They read the log and said it was good. G'wan Kit your quiddin'.

After the youngsters turned in we sat on the porch and watched the spiders and bugs. When you can't think of anything else its all-ways safe to watch the spiders. . . .

Saturday, August 5th, 1911

. . . Mr. Wachs contracted a severe cold in the ear and when we arrived this afternoon he was trying his 'steenth home made remedy. Some[one] tells him that their second cousin, twice removed had cured an earache by rubbing oil in it. So Walt ups and smears oil on his ear. Next, someone tells him that their fathers, sisters, uncles son's fourth cousin by marriage always used thus and so. Walt, he's willing so he gives that a show. After the rummy keeps that [up] seven or eight hours he gets wise and goes to the nurse. . . .

The following is original if nothing else and we print it with due apologies to the author of "The Charge of the Light Brigade."

THE CHARGE OF THE FIVE HUNGERS

'Cross the field, 'cross the field
'Cross the field, onward.
Towards the dining room hall.
Ran the five hungers.
"Forward" the bugle calls.
Rousing them, large and small.
So on to the dining room,
Rush the five hungers.

"Forward the U-B-Y-'s"
Each with the other vies
To reach first the honored prize
Theirs not to reason why
No wind to make reply
Theirs but to eat and die,
So on to the hall of grub
Charge the five hungers. . .

Spuds to the right of them
Hash to the left of them
Beans in front of them.
Beckoned and greeted.
But worn from their awful run,
Eating was not such fun,
They who had run so fleet
Sat and watched others eat,
Poor Five Hungers.

Monday, August 7th, 1911

. . . There was a Jewish pitnit at Willow Beach and San Wiener and
Rube attended — they say they had a great time — well why should'nt they they
are both good looking and have good habits, make a good appearance and look
like ready money. I'll bet the girls just about broke a leg trying to get on the floor
with them —Sarcasm: Rube looks like a long stale drink and Sanny is too bold
and forward for any good use. . . .

Wednesday, August 9th, 1911

. . . Mr. Walter Wachs accompanied by three young ladies who's names
we mercifully withold walked in to Camp from 105th Street. We certainly must
admire the girls staying powers and pluck and think its a fine stunt- for other
people, Gosh -what — these mortals be. The girls all took turns in taking care of
Wachs and they arrived in Camp very tired but happy. . . .
   Miss Malvine Jacobs was out tonight with a couple of friends. We had a
good laff when one of the girls said that our tent was wider than theirs. Mr.
Rippner understood her to say whiter, and he had awful visions for a while of
how the girls tent must look as we knew perfectly well that nothing outside of a
coal bin was darker than our tent. Explanations followed and everything was
straightened out.

Friday, August 11th, 1911

. . . These following works of art are the contribution of Mr. Is Rube
Levan — No comments please.

There is a young fellow named Sam,
For just one girl he give a ——— continental
He talks of her when he eats.
And also when he sleeps
And whenever else he can.

There was a young man called Rip,
The scales about 140 he'd tip
He writes up the log
And eats like a hog.
Some mornin' he'll wake up with the pip.

There is a young fellow named Shane,
In my side he gives me a pain.
With his 180 pounds.
And his five foot around.
He's as big as a *young* growing train.

Monday, August 14th, 1911

. . . Had a big bon fire at the beach and also had a marshmellow roast which made a decided hit with the Kids. Some of the older folks sang (?) Yiddish songs —but even that couldn't spoil the evening. Miss Spitz can see a resemblance to some genius in every long haired, crack voiced amatuer thats got nerve enuff to get up and perform. . . .

Wednesday, August 16th, 1911

. . . Turned in about 11:40 and about 1:00 A.M. the boys of the two camps were awakened and invited to an evening dress dance at one of the cottages. It was very warm and one might say almost blazing hot but that only added to the zest. Eight of the boys of the tents were in attendance and we counted eight pairs of trousers and one shirt and one sweater in the bunch. It was very informal. We had a rousing time for about half an hour and the music was grand. Our Primma Donna hit high C at least a half dozen times; Strong liquid refreshments were served by Miss Stearn. Great time and awful, exciting, Miss Spitz did a marathon in order to get Charley Dietz. We left but the others continued the festivities and when we awoke in the cold grey dawn of the morning after we found most of the Leaders still having a great time.

SOME NIGHT.

Thursday, August 17th, 1911

Oh what a tired woe-begone bunch that was this morning. No they were'nt tired — they were past that — paralized would somewhere describe it.

The participants of the midnight revel were all presented with Hero Medals today. They are of solid paper, wrought with pink and brown baby ribbon. . . .

This afternoon Pewee Blum, Cora Lederer and Fanny Spitz rowed to Euclid Beach to see Atwood. Had a fine time and it is very deserving of mention because of the fact that Miss S — got sea sick. . . .

Saturday, August 19th, 1911

. . . Miss Tina Bernstein has joined our happy family and she certainly fits in right this week. We need some level headed people here to control these flighty never-say-stop girl leaders who are holding forth out here at present, (I wonder who he means)

Take all of your sewing to Al Kohn — he's good -Please take notice of the nifty patch in the back of Al's trousers — All hand sewing too. . . .

Sunday, August 20th, 1911

. . . We have in our midst this week the "Scandal Pair" self styled, alias Martha Hahn as "Larry" and Hermine August as "Annette Kellerman" As a batter Miss Hahn is a wonder and getting better every minute and when it comes to swimming Miss August is also some Shakes. Sad to relate Miss August lost her title and dignity this afternoon, when she ate more water than was good for her and got a pain in the side and had to drink lots of booze to overcome it. Question: Why is it some people can swallow water and get sick and then get a bottle more or less of booze and get well. The Scandal Pair will now give way to the Highball triplets — Larry, Tom and Jerry.

Leo Neumark is some batter — that is he's pie for the pitcher. (Beat you at your own game, didn't I) We feel sure that Leo could bat at least fifty in the K.M. league. . . .

Miss Mollie Stern relates that she and Alex and Miss Bernstein were bawled out for daring to suggest to one of our lady patrons that it would be no more than proper that she make her bed before she left. Better send 'em a written note forty eight hours in advance after this. The idea trying to make some of our Grand Dames work. Why they can do that at home. . . .

As we predicted earlier the Leaders of this week have been simply bully. They are everything good that we have called all the others and then some. They have made this week one of the very best of the whole season and we are simply tickled to death to learn that nearly all will remain for another week. . . .

Monday, August 21st, 1911

. . . Brownie Einstein has got the proper method of toasting He tucks the stick under his arm, shoves the end in the general direction of the fire and then calmly faces the other way. Of course, he hits the ashes and the dirt with the marshmellows occasionaly — But who cares —Not the Kids. . . .

Miss Hermine August in a long semi fitted Empire model rain coat led a chorus in an attempt to sing "John Brown's Body" The silent parts were beautifully rendered, the chorus broke up because there werent enuff silent spots. . . .

. . . "Zuck" Moss is also out tonight and we went down to the point, built a fire and then "Zuck" proceeded to form a quartette. We finally did get one going as follows:

Hermine August   — Horrible
Fanny Spitz   — Terrible
Al Kohn   — Worse
Harry Rippner   — Rotten

Even Zuck gave us up and believe me when he says its no use you might as well quit. On the level, tho we think Miss August has awful sweet voice — She ought to do some thing with it — can it — or have it irrigated. . . .

Wednesday, August 23rd, 1911

. . . Little Elsie the "Belle of Camp Wise" promenaded around the ball room floor with Rube and Rip: but becoming disgusted with the crowd, she asked to be taken home. Went to the Euclid Beach on two Camp Wise Autos (?) Mae didn't care to go Did you Mae? When we got to the Beach we had a perfectly grand time watching the other folks dance. There wasn't a real shirt or collar in the bunch and we were consequently barred. We didn't want to dance anyway you understand that. . . .

Great night but just the same we were exceedingly tickeled to hit our little beds and say our "Now I lay me". . . .

Thursday, August 24th, 1911

. . . Miss Mae Oppenheimer worn out by the strenuous exertions of the past few days, slept this afternoon. Thats the true Camp Wise spirit all right, all right sleep all afternoon so that you can stay up all night.

Ye editor is on duty all night tonight and the events are complete up to 9:00 P.M. at which Mr. Levy kindly called up and posted us. We are writing this in the midst of an intense, awful stillness, it is past midnight, the witch hour and the clock is slowly ticking off the seconds. On all sides is darkness intense and inpenetrable and as we sit and ponder there flashes insistently thro our mind, over and over again the old, old rythm-"Sleep, thou art a blessed thing, beloved from pole to pole" My kingdom for a bed.

Sweet Dreams.

Friday, August 25th, 1911

. . . The Nottingham Citizens Band came over tonight and regaled us with some splendid selection. Doc filled in as a drum player and proved to be the main attraction. . . .

Sunday, August 27th, 1911

At last the day for which we hoped and longed while shunning and dreading is upon us. . . . Right after breakfast we started in to fix up Camp for the board meeting in the afternoon. Most of the boys helped clean the porch, while Rube and Rip set off to gather thorn apples and oak leaves. Did you ever pick thorn apples? Fine job — each individual branch has a thousand thorns more or less and every time you cut down one twig — you run a few hundred thorns into yourself. We picked maple leaves instead of oak leaves — but you can hardly blame that on us. Professor of Agriculture Charles Dietz, Esquire pointed them out to us.

Then we went over and helped Hermine August and Mae Oppenheimer clean up the hospital. We did some job — scrubbed every inch and washed all the windows and silver ware and cut glass. We think that Mae ought to develope into a great help to her mother. Hermine bossed the job and more than that she also worked darn hard. Should have seen Rube on his hands and knees mopping the floor. After working on this for about an hour and half you can bet we can appreciate what it means when they say that "womens work is never done" Hermine had just put on a clean white dress two days before the day before yesterday, but you should have seen it after we were finished, there were a few white spots — but very few. Then sweet Albert Kohn came over and we cleaned the porch and vicinity. Vicinity includes the girls and ourselves — Oh yes Al's some sprinkler. . . .

. . . Then rehearsal — and it wasn't so awful rotten — tho the Lord knows it was bad enuff. . . .

. . . We were thro at 4:00 o'clock and when we got out we were a surprised bunch — there was all of 250 to 300 visitors strolling around, and one side of the grounds was full of autos. . . . The girls gave a May Pole dance which was very, very pretty.

The Board meeting was then called to order and from all accounts it must have been a very satisfactory meeting. Miss Martha Hahn said that she was going to propose that the board go on record as being in favor of midnight lunches, and onion sandwiches. . .

At 8:15 — Professor Gene Geismer rang the bell and sent out "Reggie" Kohn to call the boys to school. An immense crowd greeted us. The vast auditorium was literally packed with a cheering, laughing concourse of people. The porches and all the surroundings Territory was also filled with people. The play was an assured success even before it started.

TITLE   —   School Days
TIME   —   Present
SCENE   —   Camp Wise on the Lake

CAST

Professor Gene Geismer   *An old fashioned school teacher with an in-growing sense of humor and out growing ego.*

"Supervisor" Phil Leon   *A german inspector, with a limburger accent and a funny face.*

"Lizzie" Levan   *Otherwise Rube — a peroxide blond, with a cracked voice and a bum shape.*

"Hiam" Furman   *Little Jewish boy — with a funny face and very good at figures (certain Kind)*

Reggie "Kohn"   *A dear gentle little lad, with lots of brain and no "verstand" —made to be swatted by the tuff guy.*

Alex Yensen   *He bane be a Sweedish boy — and also the dunce, with a nutty look and a silly whistle.*

"Pagliaco" Blum   *Little de Italiena boy-with a wop face (natural), and lots of motion.*

"Faunterloy" Denby   *Cant guess — Think he's H'Inglishman — Deep voice and good singer (in practice.)*

"Rastus" Grossman   *Doc — put in to prompt teacher and the inspector.*

Wachs   *An pupil*

Harold Einstein   *A precosious youngster — who gets in bad.*

"Young Jack Johnson"   *Warsaw — Davy with his face blackened.*

"Muggsy" Rip   *A real tuff guy — wid a tuff look and spits nickels.*

The play was a great success and even tho we did forget about one half of our lines nobody knew any better. . . .

The girls also put on a play — but coming as it did after such a brilliant show as ours, and after such a wonderful exhibition of acting it fell flat. We will say this —the girls were very pretty, they certainly look cute in short dresses and the scenery was fine. Ask Ida Schott she will tell you the same thing.

The "dear" little tinderdarten dirls" were supposed to pretend to forget some of their lines. The only trouble was that they overdone it — and really did forget — too realistic girls.

Hermine August as "topsy" certainly was a peach. When she grows up, we believe she will be some actor.

TITLE   —   A day in Ida Schott's nursery for antiquated girls.
TIME   —   Daytime
PLACE   —   Any old place where people will listen.

CAST

Martha Hahn	*Little Bo Peep*
Hermine August	*Topsy*
Mae Oppenheimer	*Dotty Dimples*
Molly Stearn	*Idala*
Tina Bernstein	*Little Eva*
Ida Schott	*Teacher*

None of the girls were real bad — but some more so than others. . . .

Sat around the porch and told each other how good we were and tried to cheer up the girls (no they weren't mad)

If you have ever seen a more tired conglomeration of mortals. than those who lay around that porch tonight. You might label them. We had put in one awful strenuous day and can't say that we're sorry its over. . . .

It has been a great day, a fitting climax to a wonderful season and we are all glad to have been here and taken part in it. Also, we are darn glad that we're not troubled with insomnia tonight.

Monday, August 28, 1911

. . . Ate our last meal at the hotel this morning and believe us it was a sorrowful meal — every way you look at it — temperamentally and in quantity. Even the sweet presence of our dear "ittle tinderdarten chillen" couldn't cheer us up. . . .

Got the 10:00 o'clock car into town this morning and said our last good-bye to Mae Oppenheimer and Hermine August and Miss Bernstein and Dora Mendelsohn. The rest will still be here tonight. So long girls — Auf Wiedersehen. . . .

Came out on the 6:30 car from town and found a goodly supply of the leaders still there — eating. Went over and fixed up the tent and then back to the hotel in time to get in on the desert.

After supper we repaired to the dance hall and then it started.

First on the programme was a little dance —music by Professor Doc Grossman. Then some musical numbers. At about 8:00 Mr. Is Shane brought his 200 pound carcass onto the floor and at 8:30 Mr. Jo Denby arrived and immediately favored us with a song. It's a new song never heard out here before, name is "My Hero." Everybody had important business and when Denby finished he was all alone in the room. Mr. Wise and Mrs. Wise arrived about this time and then we had a very interesting little game of medicine ball with a pumpkin. Pumpkin broke and we started another nice quiet little game, of which we don't know the name but goes like this: Some one stands up against the wall and all the rest throw a nice, hard boxing glove at you. When you guess who throws it, then that party is "it." No lives lost and nobody got cold feet. In fact, Ida Schott liked it so well that she didn't try to guess. Wasn't that it Miss S., or *couldn't* you guess? Then we played Jerusalem. Mollie Stearn by virtue of running rings around one chair won out. . . . Then we had an apple race — tied apples on strings and suspended them from the ceiling and the one who ate his whole apple first, without using his hands or feet, got the prize. Doc won. He got the prize. It was three cheers. . . .

At about 12:— o'clock we bade all of our friends good-bye and sang a very pathetic and original little song in farewell — entitled GOOD NIGHT LADIES — on sale in all music stores. We had one grand old time tonight — just how good, it is hard to explain — everyone got in it and we ended up in great style.

So endeth officially the Camp Wise Season of 1911. In our opinion it has been the best and most successful, without exception, since the opening of the institution. Working under a terrific handicap, the Camp has nevertheless come thro with flying colors. The leaders have been all enthusiastic, and tireless and were all blessed with cast iron stomachs. On behalf of Camp U.B.Y.'s and we are sure we voice the sentiments of our neighbors Camp O'luvus, we wish to thank the heads of this institution, who make our stay possible. It has been a glorious summer and well spent. Good bye until next summer.

Alliwise is to Camp Wise what reunions are to high school and college classes. At least so it was when it started over seven decades ago. For its members, the spirit of Camp Wise remains bright and its ambience of nature and camping life still alluring. Alliwise — the name is a blend of Alliance and Camp Wise — began in 1916 with a post-summer weekend to provide dedicated senior graduates with the opportunity to refresh their recollections of earlier camp days.

Alliwise over the years has expanded its activities to meetings year-round, not just social but supportive of many service organizations, including first and foremost, the Camp Wise scholarship program. All of this is touched on in the account prepared by Al Brown. In addition, the chronicle section of the volume includes a number of entries drawn from the Alliwise newsletter, first printed in 1931 as The Gong, which featured the whereabouts of friends, their engagements and weddings (many of the married first met at Camp Wise), and informal sketches of leading members in the Camp-Alliwise union.

Members of Alliwise have done more than merely recall the "House of Happiness." As their record briefly described here shows they have enriched and today still nourish life at Camp Wise.

Alliwise

Albert M. Brown

At the 50th Anniversary of the Council Educational Alliance in March, 1948, George B. Mayer, speaking of Camp Wise, made the following remarks about Alliwise:

> Always interested in finding newer and better ways in which to render more service to its members, the Alliance encouraged groups to attend Camp Wise even after they were too old for the regular camp season. This laid the basis for the organization known as Alliwise, which for years conducted a week in camp after the regular season closed. This is one of the few such groups which exist in connection with any similar settlement house in the country.

The camp season had ended in 1916 when a few Senior Club members of the Alliance asked permission to use Camp Wise over the Labor Day weekend. Walter Leo Solomon, head worker of the Alliance that year, spearheaded the idea, along with Senior members Leo Ascherman, Dan Wasserman, Harry Lipson, Eli Drucker, Aaron Goldman, Sam Brown, Sam Rose, Sidney Katzman, Hy Gittelson, Jack Gittelson, Charles Shaffer, Charles Koch, and Harry Blachman.

Then in 1918 the weekend idea was expanded to a full week, which began the day after the regular season ended. A group of 60 young adults, Senior Club members, college students, and working men and women, all associated with the Alliance, spent a most enjoyable week at Camp Wise.

The name of the "week" came quite naturally to be known as *Alliwise*, a combination of *Alliance* and *Wise*. Ida Schott and Mr. Solomon were the older adult leaders supervising the group. From that week of camping there emerged a year-round organization, engaged in social and philanthropic activities. As of today, there are over 700 members, many of them leaders in community endeavors.

Alliwise week was a blend of fun, friendship, congeniality, and serious discussions on politics, current events, and philosophical problems. Since they no longer use Camp Wise for the week, that same spirit still prevails at the annual weekend at Hiram House camp in the fall each year, and at all the trips elsewhere. But besides being a social group, Alliwise prides itself on its generosity and assistance to the Greater Cleveland community, both Jewish and non-Jewish. The organization donates to the Jewish Community Center Camp Scholarships, Jewish Welfare Fund, United Way campaigns, Society for Crippled Children, Julie Kravitz Fund Run for Israel, Bellefaire Workshop, the Hugo Mahrer Chapel at Halle Park, and the Ida Schott Golden Age Fund.

The members have a tradition of long-standing, close friendships, many romances, and strong loyalty to Alliwise. Romances did flourish through the years at Alliwise, and some even resulted in marriages. Rumor has it that Ida Schott, in her innocent, quiet, unassuming manner, may have had some hand in promoting, encouraging, even arranging some of these recorded marriages. Many others may never have been entered in Alliwise unofficial records. Here are just a few:

Harry and Elsie Albert	Hy and Henrietta Gittelson
Charles and Esther Ascherman	Jack and Lena Gittelson
Leo and Marie Ascherman	Myer and Gus Givelber
Harry and Sarah Blachman	Aaron and Dena Goldman
Sam and Bertha Brown	Art and Mitzie Hirsch
Irwin and Sylvia Dann	Charles and Lillian Koch
Jonas and Bea Deutsch	Harry and Blanche Leutenberg
Shy and Julie Diamond	Harry and Lillian Levine
Jack and Lena Franklin	Hugo and Rose Mahrer
Al and Augusta Gilman	Charles and Fay Udelf

The Alliwise newsletter, *The Gong*, is published each month and has been put together almost from the very beginning by Blanche and Harry Leutenberg. *The Gong* keeps its members all over the country well-posted on events and personal stories.

There are men and women in Greater Cleveland, and indeed in all parts of the country, who date their membership in Alliwise as far back as 1916. Leo Ascherman and Harry Blachman are two of the originals. Ida Schott is said to have attended every Alliwise week from 1920, the year she was appointed Associate Director of the Alliance, to the early 50's. Although she was always considered the unofficial director of Alliwise camp week, the programs of the entire week were planned well in advance by committees of Alliwise in town.

Practically every hour of every day for that one week was scheduled long before the camp trip — swimming, softball games, volleyball, hikes, nature lore, campfires, archery, ping-pong, badminton, golf putting, song sessions, dancing, and, of course, good food! The mock election campaigns were always hilarious events. These mock elections were really rehearsals for the more serious election of Alliwise officers to be held later in town.

The annual musical or play was well rehearsed in town during the year so that the performance at Alliwise was polished and very professional. My best recollection of a good dramatic show at Alliwise goes back to 1928, when we presented that popular one-act play, "The Valiant," by Robert Middlemass and Holworth Hall, with its famous closing line from Shakespeare's "Julius Caesar" — "Cowards die many times before their deaths; the valiant never taste of death but once. . ."

The following summer, encouraged by the response to "The Valiant," we decided to present the tough newspaper play, "The Front Page," by Charles McArthur and Ben Hecht. We rehearsed the play diligently in town and looked forward to the Alliwise presentation. However, after Ida Schott and Walter Leo Solomon saw the final rehearsal at camp, they objected to some of the language, and we had to omit the most important lines in the play. But we "valiantly," albeit reluctantly, did a cleaned-up version and called it "The Back Page." That's show biz!

Whenever there were oldtimers' reunions of Alliwise, they would never be complete without these performances:

Leon Gaines doing an impression of George Arliss in "The Green Goddess" (better than the original!)

Leo Ascherman giving his Annual House Congress speech

Ezra Shapiro singing "Ey-ukhnyem" ("The Volga Boatman")

Bea Deutsch playing the piano so skillfully, with husband, Jonas, expertly turning the pages

Irv Dann reciting lines from "White Cargo"

Maury Antine telling ghost stories

Dan Wasserman reading from Plato

Hy and Jack Gittelson singing their "off-key" duet

Sarah Blachman singing any song that husband Harry wrote

Joe Bernay giving impressions and singing Yiddish songs

Lou Lieder with some of his prize poetry, such as:
>   Eli Rose went for a walk
>   And sat upon a cactus stalk,
>   In order to avoid small talk
>   Eli Rose!

George Washington is said to have been the first in war, first in peace, and first in the hearts of his countrymen. . . . But Leo Ascherman was the Alliance House Congress president at the first Alliance gathering and then first president of Alliwise. A few of the presidents following Ascherman, as they come to mind, were: Ben Antine, Sol Abrams, Jack Berman, Nate Berman, Sid Bailus, Morry Feld, Jerry Fine, Joe Krosin, Jonas Deutsch, Arthur Hirsch, Hy Paris, Al Mayerson, Sonny Nagelbush, Bernie Newmark, Sam Frager, Paul Wolfson, Bernie Wiener, Shia Shapiro, Sam Levine, Sally Levine, Irving Tuffyas, Ben Weltman, George Solomon, Arnold Soroky, Sam Zelvy, Robert Zelvy, Joe Bernay, Al Leventhal, Oscar Weinstein, Al Guthoff, Fritzi Henkin, and Morris Fierman.

Many members of Alliwise went on to become well-known professional and business executives in Cleveland and elsewhere. In sports, there were two in particular: Philip "Doc" Wolfe, star quarterback of Western Reserve University, physical education director of the Alliance, coach and first director of Camp Alliance; and Abe "Yabo" Greenspan, all-Ohio basketball player from Ohio State and athletic director at the Kinsman Branch of Council Educational Alliance.

It was "Yabo" who wrote that Alliwise theme song:

> Alliwise is so grand, O! believe me,
> We'll ne'er forget what it means;
> The days so bright,
> Full of delight,
> Each moment filled with bliss;
> And when Alliwise days are gone,
> Make believe — don't let on,
> Think of the days we spent together;
> Just recall all the fun
> And your blues will be gone,
> Rah! Rah! for A-L-L-I-W-I-S-E!

THE GONG

JULY 1988

ALLIWISE ASSOCIATION

YOU ASKED FOR IT !

ALLIWISE PICNIC

Sunday, August 14, 1988

Anisfield Day Camp

For Alliwise Members
And their Families

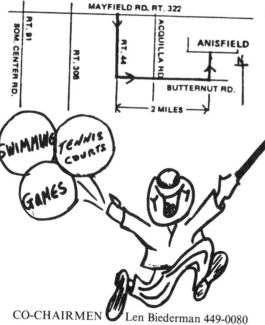

PARK ADMISSION: $2.00 PER CAR

FREE DRINKS AND ICE-CREAM

GUARDED SWIMMING POOL

POOL ACTIVITIES

11:00-GATE OPENS
  BRING YOUR LUNCH
1:00 to 4:00
  REGISTRATION
1:30-GAMES-PRIZES
5:00-DOOR PRIZE DRAWING

CO-CHAIRMEN Len Biederman 449-0080   Sam Buckantz 461-6866

Sidney Z. Vincent (1912-1982) was one of the Cleveland Jewish community's distinguished professional leaders. His contributions, notably in community relations and Jewish culture and education, reached beyond his home city to national and international levels. Much of what he contributed is told in his autobiography, Personal and Professional, Memoirs of a Life in Community Service *(Cleveland, 1982), which he wrote after retiring in 1975 as executive director of the Jewish Community Federation of Cleveland.*

Sidney Vincent began his career modestly, though no less importantly, as a teacher of English in the Cleveland public school system. He influenced many students, who recall with pleasure their classes with him at Glenville High School. While still a teacher, he began his entry into Jewish communal service by working at Camp Wise during the summer months. His eight years there as a leader and assistant director were marked by enthusiasm, program creativity, and administrative skills, especially in the early war years when the camp was left without experienced personnel who had entered the military. Only willing but apprentice teenagers, not much older than the campers, remained available as staff, but the Painesville camp still carried on, in no small measure due to Sid's commitment.

These pages from the Vincent autobiography tell of a difficult period in Camp Wise history, enriched by his personal observations. Curiously, Sid's description of the camp on page 114 differs in some details from that in the Plain Dealer *description on page 17. The account is reprinted here with the permission of his wife, Ruth Vincent.*

Mid-Years at
Camp Wise
1935-1943

Sidney Z. Vincent

The open part of my calendar was now the summer, but Joe Rose and Leon Weil together fixed that. The entire Rose family (three fellows and three girls) was talented, handsome, vital—and into everything. Joe was particularly charming, the first Freudian in our circle, a free spirit who exuded an aura of daring and novelty and yet was totally dedicated to community responsibilities. He practically commanded me, soon after I had settled down in a teaching career, to devote my summers to working at Camp Wise, the communal camp located at that time about five miles east of Painesville, on Lake Erie. At his prompting, I went to see the president of Camp Wise, Leon Weil, who engaged me on the spot as boys' worker.

It seemed like a good if somewhat insane deal all around. The camp got my services at a price they could afford during the Depression — nothing. I got bed and board for the summer; and Ruth, who of course was working (as secretary to Herbert Buckman, then the Commissioner of Public Hall and Stadium), became a welcome guest on weekends, or whenever she could make it out to camp. So, as Leon pointed out in his dry, sardonic manner, I was really being richly rewarded in view of the immense savings I could effect during the summer. Moreover, from the camp standpoint hiring me was taking quite a chance. Since I had never so much as seen any camp for children, I hadn't the foggiest notion of how it should operate.

Joe and Leon were prepared to deal with my ignorance. The camp was largely run by volunteers, which explained why my interview and instant hiring were by a layman. Activities during the off season were in the hands of a remarkable organization known as the Camp Wise Crew, made up of those who had served as volunteer leaders in previous years. What a crew they were! During the winter they ran a ten-week institute for those who wished to volunteer their services for the coming summer, teaching camp philosophy, skills, ways of handling kids, and mounting a fine social program for good measure. Instructors were mostly camp alumni, supplemented from time to time by faculty members from the School of Applied Social Science, who for the most part also volunteered their services. The result was a marvelous combination of hard work and sheer fun — always a winning trick. Dorothy Wahl and Dave Apple and Elmer Louis and literally dozens of others who later distinguished themselves in teaching and social service and community work brought imagination and zest and discipline to the sessions. The leaders-to- be responded with almost perfect attendance and high enthusiasm.

Unlike the permanent staff that came out for the entire summer, the leaders served for only a single trip of two weeks. They were selected by the Crew after rigorous examination to determine how well they met the institute's high standards — for voluntary positions! Maybe nostalgia distorts my memory, and the organization was less remarkable than I remember it. But I don't really believe that. So many of us learned what creativity and what fun there could be in communal service. So many communal leaders began their careers of distinguished service at Camp Wise.

Camp Wise had its weak points. In the late thirties, Industrial Rayon Corporation built its factory directly across the road. It permanently cut off all hiking toward the east, the only open direction, and destroyed any illusion of a rural setting. When the wind was from the east, you could smell the factory as well as see it. Structurally, too, Camp Wise was a far cry from modern ideas of what a camp should be. It consisted of four large wooden cottages, each containing four living units surrounding a recreation hall and a kitchen, all constructed in a style more appropriate for a commercial resort than a kids' camp dedicated to roughing it in the unspoiled outdoors. In addition, there were four tents for the older boys and three for the older girls, all erected on cement slabs. Each contained ten cots. Leaders slept on mattresses, but the kids had straw ticks, excellent for young bedwetters but a nuisance to empty and refill every two weeks for each of the five camp trips. The lake was beautiful for sunsets and general viewing but rotten for swimming. It was already quite polluted, and much of the time the waves were too violent to permit any kind of swimming instruction. Often we had to call off the regular swim period, even in sunny weather.

The problems were not only physical. In the early years two of the large cottages were given over for use by mothers and babies, which complicated schedule-making and programming, particularly when some mamas came out to camp not only with their babies but with older children. Inevitably, they tried to keep tabs on their kids, embarrassing them and bringing on occasional homesick upsets in other campers.

We shared the property with Camp Henry Baker, just across a ravine formed by a little creek. Baker was the summer camp of the Council Educational Alliance, eventually to become the Jewish Community Center in 1948. There was a good deal of cooperation between the two camps, but also considerable rivalry. Baker's staff was far more professional in their approach than ours, since they were trained social workers who were for the most part year-round employees of the Council. We were a hit-or-miss gang, thrown together each year, of teachers and odds and ends of talent, some still college students, recruited pretty much as I had been. The difference showed up in programming.

During my first couple of years we used the "five day activity" system, with kids choosing twice during their two-week trip from a smorgasbord of possible offerings (dramatics, campcraft, handcraft, exploring, etc.) largely reflecting the skills and the interests of the leaders of the particular trip. The Henry Baker people were patronizing about such lack of sophistication. They ran their camp on the "project" principle, they informed us. Each tent or cottage developed a central idea (build a treehouse, develop a kibbutz, create a nature trail, construct an Indian village, etc.) aimed at uniting the group. Though in the process they taught all kinds of skills, the really important objective, they informed us, was to realize well-defined (and certainly frequently defined) social and personal achievement goals. Relationships, self-understanding — *that* was the ticket.

We argued nightly, when leaders of both camps got together, over what semed to be our differing approaches. The Wise defense rested on the superiority of vigorous practice over stuffy theory. As the years went on, the differences between us eroded, until finally the two camps were merged. As is so often the case, we all overestimated the importance of technique. The genius of camp lay elsewhere.

Much of it, at least as far as Camp Wise was concerned, revolved around its director, Albert (Spunk) Kinoy. A physical education teacher in a New York high school who earlier had been an employee of the local Council Educational Alliance, he was a perfect choice to head the camp. He was in his mid-forties in 1935 when I first met him, short, husky, with wisps of the little hair left to him floating in the breeze, forever puffing comfortably on his pipe. Spunk was the classic liberal, in the best sense of that now suspect term. He never really got much involved in programming, conceiving his job to be encouraging and backing up and developing the members of his staff responsible for the actual work, applauding their successes and gently helping them to evaluate and learn from their failures. He created an atmosphere of complete confidence in our efforts so that, although he almost never made demands on us, we were ready to knock ourselves out to justify his trust. All of us, following his example, developed an intense closeness and got to know and share one another's problems in a way more like a family relationship than a working relationship. His older son, Arthur, now a professor of constitutional law at Rutgers University and a nationally known legal authority, came with him for two summers and developed, at the age of seventeen, into one of our most imaginative leaders. His other son, Ernest, was too young to be a leader and spent his summers at another camp. It was a loss to us, since he has become one of the nation's most creative writers for television. Spunk's wife, Sarah Jane, ran her own camp in the East, but occasionally she too visited us and also became part of the camp family.

How to capture the spirit of those days? The two hundred campers each two-week trip (one thousand for the summer) were mostly from poor families, a good many of them paying nothing at all. We on the staff were terribly conscious of emerging from an earlier stage of camp history, when the objective was primarily to provide two weeks of fresh air and good food, with a program emphasizing sports. We took all that for granted, but we were after ''higher'' objectives. Baseball, for example, was not quite a necessary evil, but it also was not to be an important concern. Developing the personality and exploring the world of the outdoors and learning to ''relate'' were more vital goals, as was a new but passionate emphasis on Jewish commitment. The positive results of our work, when things went right, were demonstrated in the contrast between the raggedy lines of kids at initial registration, many of them teary-eyed and homesick, and the gang of knowledgeable camp veterans two weeks later, lustily singing camp songs and shouting vows of eternal friendship. In an astonishing number of cases, those predictions really came true.

During my first summer at camp I was thrown abruptly into responsibilities despite my lack of experience. Spunk was always ten days late in arriving because the New York schools let out that long after camp opened. Moreover, that first year he came down with gall bladder trouble that knocked him out for long stretches during the summer. The major responsibility devolved on my colleague on the girls' side of the campus, Dorothy Wahl. She was a dynamo, inspiring leaders, supervising the staff, looking after the kitchen, comforting the kids, breaking me in, and generally running herself ragged until she would simply collapse for a day or two before coming back strong as ever. Her assistant, and later the top camp person, Lil Berkowitz, was a musician and, among her many other contributions, helped raise our level of musical expression from unmelodious shoutings of cheap music to some really fine singing that drew heavily on Jewish tradition and American folk songs. Alfred (Bud) Schlesinger was first a leader, then our swimming instructor, then our head boys' worker. He demonstrated what should be obvious — that competence in a skill does not necessarily guarantee ability to impart the skill to others. We had magnificent, almost professional swimmers who were terrible at teaching the kids. Bud was a good swimmer though hardly a champion. But his ability to understand kids, to work patiently with them, to tease them into ducking their heads under water was infinitely more valuable than the flashy speed demonstrations of the champs. It helped me to understand why so many athletes turn out to be poor managers or coaches, while many who barely made it in their playing careers often do a fine job of bringing out the best in others.

My own responsibilities were bounded only by my energy. Beyond my major duties in programming and supervision, I was usually the storyteller at the Friday night services in the Council Ring. I can't imagine a more inspiring setting for storytelling. The kids dressed up (which means having showered and changed to reasonably clean clothing) and were somewhat settled down by the Shabbos services. The twilight and the gathering night usually brought a cooling breeze early in the summer or a crackling council fire in the late summer trips; either set a perfect mood for spinning yarns. My background in literature stood me well, and I found I didn't have to patronize the campers. My tales came from Jewish tradition, in stories like "If Not Higher" by I. L. Peretz; or in dramatic yarns like "Zodomirsky's Duel" by Dumas, or Robert Louis Stevenson's "The Suicide Club," or Stockton's "The Lady and the Tiger." Years later I would use them again as bedtime stories for my grandsons. I never had much use for fairy stories or sweet good night tales. My aim for both campers and grandchildren was to provide a vivid story, preferably winding up with some question to brood about. It may have been bad psychology to stimulate my listeners instead of singing a lullaby, but the subsequent discussions before they settled into sleep were good for my soul. And maybe theirs too.

Occasionally Lil wasn't around to lead the singing, and I filled in with my one contribution — a simple little Israeli song called "Shmor." It had only three words for the kids to remember: "Shmor shimru achim," meaning "On guard, fellows." It was the admonition, as I dramatically explained, of Jewish watchmen guarding new settlements in Eretz Yisroel. The song had other verses, but they consisted of humming or whistling the tune without words. Then came the climax. The last verse was "sung" silently till the final explosive burst of "Shmor!" This was supposed to erupt in unison but usually someone got in a beat early—or late. That always brought down the house. I became so identified with my one-song repertoire that I was frequently known seriously by the kids and jestingly by the leaders as "Shmor."

On a higher (or lower) musical note, I also had starring roles in our Leaders Night operetta — if that is the right word for what we produced. It was performed the last Sunday night of each trip and was always a more or less garbled version of a Gilbert and Sullivan operetta. (We more accurately referred to it as a "Garber and Solomon" presentation.) Over the years, we alternated among *Trial by Jury*, *The Mikado*, *Pinafore*, and *Pirates of Penzance*. I built up quite a repertory of lead roles and, except for Bud Schlesinger, whose voice was even worse than mine, developed into one of the outstanding monotones of the performances. But the kids loved it and so did the leaders, even though they came to the few rehearsals so exhausted that they had to call on new reserves of energy to get through the sessions.

Besides, rehearsal time cut into "cliffing." Camp Wise was right on Lake Erie, with a cliff rising perhaps thirty feet above the beach. At night, after the kids were asleep and when there were no meetings, the leaders would wander off in couples to highly private spots along the cliff, being careful to take camp blankets with them. The aim, I presume, was to meditate on the rolling breakers below.

My responsibility was to cut short those meditations at midnight. Armed with a flashlight aimed mostly at the sky and accompanied for protection by another staff member, I would approach the cliff area, but not too close. When various lumps moved and divided into two separate bodies, we would cough discreetly and observe into the darkness that bedtime had come. We always rounded up the leaders as the day's final staff duty. We relied on the bed count to ensure that the leaders had enough sleep to face up to the demanding schedule with the kids the next day. But I would hate to guarantee that they all stayed put after we on the staff went to bed.

No account of Camp Wise during the four decades of its stay at the Painesville location would be complete without mention of the two personalities who anchored the entire period. One was the caretaker, George Jackson. Tall, lean, all muscle, with a corncob pipe forever dangling from his mouth, absolutely unperturbable, he gloried in the legend that George can do anything. We never found any blueprints for the water or sewage or electricity systems; evidently they existed only in George's mind. God knows what would have happened if at any time during those decades he had had to be replaced. He hauled everything, patched everything, redesigned everything, while cheerfully agreeing that he was a master painter, carpenter, electrician, plumber, or what not. Nothing stumped him.

One year, two of us were in the mothers' cottage, getting things ready for camp opening the next day, when a couple of rocks bigger than grapefruit came smashing through the roof and landed a few yards from us. We were horrified but George wasn't. He came walking up from the beach, where he had been blasting rocks to clear the bathing area, surveyed the damage, scratched his head, puffed on his pipe, and repeated his favorite comment on all the world's happenings: "Gol dang dern."

He did get his comeuppance once, however. One of the attractive features of camp was its medical department. In addition to a full-time nurse, we also had, until the war changed things, a live-in doctor, usually a former leader who had just completed his residency at a hospital and welcomed a summer relaxing at camp before going into private practice.

A succession of men who later became distinguished physicians served in the post, but at camp their prime objective was fun. One summer, Dr. Zoltan Klein was our physician. A relatively short and slight fellow, he had been a member of the wrestling team at Western Reserve University. Somehow, he and George got to talking about wrestling skills, and George allowed as how none of them there college fellows with their vague theories would have much show against the natural skill and sheer strength that he represented. Zoltan thought otherwise, so just for the hell of it, they put on an impromptu wrestling match. George was on his back in nothing flat. He absolutely couldn't believe it. He tried again, with the same results. You could see a lifetime of conviction tottering. Evidently there *was* something, after all, to that shadowy world of sophisticated learning. But the only comment he made was, "Gol dang dern."

The other significant figure was Hugo Mahrer — Uncle Hugo to everybody.

He had been associated with the camp for many years before my time, having served it in every conceivable capacity. He demonstrated classically what a volunteer can mean to community service. He held a responsible position in town, but almost every weekend and many evenings, often with his wife Rose, he would rush out to camp, where we would unmercifully exploit his tremendous skills and knowledge of camp-craft and nature lore. Nor was that all. He was probably the only man whose judgment on maintenance problems George Jackson really respected, so that Hugo for many years served as a kind of overseer to the physical well-being and upgrading of every aspect of camp. Moreover, he had a marvelous way with kids both as a leader of groups and as a friend to those loners who had difficulty relating to anyone else.

Although Hugo best exemplified the spirit of volunteerism which was the distinctive contribution of camp, hundreds of young people from every walk of life had their first experience in community leadership at Camp Wise. Standards were high. It was a privilege to be selected as a leader, even though you were not paid. The Depression helped, of course, since we had our pick of young talent because jobs were almost impossible to find. So why not a summer at camp? As for the affluent, a tradition of serving at camp had become so deeply established that "the best" young people eagerly volunteered along with the sons and daughters of the working man and the little businessman. The result was a fine mix of the Glenville, Kinsman, and Heights crowds, in vivid contrast to the more common tendency of the country club set and "the masses" — to use the descriptive terms of the day — to go their own ways.

Each year camp ended abruptly. Spunk was due back in New York the next day, so the trustees instituted the pleasant custom of an annual meeting to honor the staff, held at the Oakwood Club on the night camp closed. What an occasion that annual meeting was! In the morning we were still workers, dressed in our shorts and *shmattes*, frantically bidding the kids goodbye while closing up camp, often after an all-night bust-up. Then a mad dash back into town, with the girls on the staff rushing off to their hairdresser appointments. That night, we all reassembled for dinner at what seemed the most posh of environments — a country club. Decked out in our best duds, hardly recognizing each other, we were wined and dined. Each member of the staff gave a brief account of the work we had been responsible for during the summer — reports that we somehow knocked out in those frantic last days. The board listened with the greatest of good will. And what a board! William C. (Bill) Treuhaft, the first professional at camp, years before, served as treasurer; Leon Weil and George Hays were the presidents during my time; Ruth Newman was the long-term registrar; Dr. Oscar Markey was our in-town medical consultant. The list of outstanding community personalities went on and on.

The next day it was all over, and we were back to "real" work. But the friendships forged during those summer months have worn well over the years. Some of my closest friends I first met at camp, and hardly a week passes, forty years later, without some reminiscence about the good days at Camp Wise.

Dedication of Halle Park, June 19, 1966. Ernie Siegler, president, Jewish Community Center, at the podium. (H)

Dedication of Halle Park. Julie Kravitz presenting testimonial to Hugo Mahrer. (H)

Dave Warshawsky recalling the first sixty years of Camp Wise at the dedication. (H)

Honoring the spirited director of Camp Wise at the Halle Park dedication, June 19, 1966. Left to right: Howard Robbins, Julie Kravitz, and Abe Bonder. (H)

Making it official. Unveiling the Halle Park tablet. Left to right: Herman Eigen, Julie Kravitz, Ernie Siegler, and Philmore Haber, representing the Halle Foundation. (H)

Sabbath services at the Hugo Mahrer Chapel conducted by campers, 1982. (D)

The Leon G. Weil Nature Trail, honoring one of Camp Wise's outstanding leaders, 1979. (D)

A chapel under the skies, which would have pleased "Uncle" Hugo, 1975. (H)

Camp Wise greets its Burton neighbors, 1972. (C)

A Camp Wise chore, rolling blankets after a sleepout, 1971.

Cycling on the Camp Wise dirt road, 1976. (D)

A big splash into the Camp Wise pool, 1980. (D)

Three in one at the playground — tennis, basketball, and volleyball, 1970. (H)

A sing-a-long after dinner with guitar instructor Joan Pashin, 1970's. (D)

Nature Study, Eyes on the Rocks, 1967. (H)

A safe way to fish in the Halle Park lake, 1970's. (D)

Budding actors in drama class, as part of the Camp Wise arts program, 1974. (D)

Fun and games at the end of the day, 1968. (H)

The Israeli presence at Camp Wise, Kfar Noar, 1970's. (D)

All join hands in Israeli dance in recreation hall, 1974. (H)

A Hebrew language class with an Israeli teacher, 1971. (H)

Sabbath candles and kiddush at Camp Wise, 1982. (D) Wienies taste better prepared over a smoky wood fire at Camp Wise, 1979. (D)

A quiet moment in the recreation hall, 1975. (D)

The decorated entrance to Craft Shack, 1972. (H)

Teaching first aid; demonstrating how to bandage a sprain, 1974. (D)

"Having a great time," — a letter home, 1973. (H)

Budding artists sharpen their craft skills, 1973. (H)

Everyone joins in this outdoor Israeli dance, 1970. (D)

Budding archers check their target, 1968. (D)

Juniors at Camp Wise on a float trip at Mohican Wilderness, 1971. (D)

The Nature Trail at Anisfield Day Camp, Mandel JCC woods, honoring Abe Bonder. Left to right:
Senator Howard Metzenbaum, Evelyn Bonder and grandchildren, Dave Apple, 1988. (D)

Accompanying the birds in an outdoor guitar lesson, 1974. (H)

A picturesque view of the Halle Park lake created by damming part of the West Branch Cuyahoga River, 1967. (H)

The World of Camp Wise, a bird's-eye view, 1972. (H)

The heart of this chronicle consists of excerpts from the minutes of the Camp Wise Association, which was incorporated late in 1907 to accept and administer the property, Stein-on-the-Lake, near Euclid Ohio, donated by industrialist Samuel D. Wise. Its management of Camp Wise, an appropriate name to this day, ended in 1948, when the Camp became an integral part of the Jewish Community Center created by the merger of several existing agencies.

Fortunately, the Association records are preserved along with other Camp papers as part of the Jewish Community Center collection in the Cleveland Jewish Archives at the Western Reserve Historical Society. These other sources included the following: The Gong, an informative newsletter with many social notes, started in 1931 by the Alliwise Association of Camp Wise graduates and supporters; minutes of the JCC camping committee; reports of the Camp professional staff; and lastly, documents written in the years prior to the establishment of Halle Park in 1966, which highlight the leadership of Herman Eigen, JCC executive director, and an ad hoc committee, named the Friends of Camp Wise, who made the new complex a reality. All of these papers contribute excerpts to the Camp chronicle. All have interest, but in the staff records are two of special note, Howard Robbins' 1943 account of the wartime farm program he directed and Abe Bonder's review of the 1957 Camp year with its personal overtones.

Over the 1907-1948 period, the Association records also change significantly in focus, starting with Eugene Geismer, its first president, and other leaders, such as William Treuhaft and Ida Schott, the doyenne of Camp Wise for many years. The Association board initially resolved practical problems involving the day-to-day operations, and then in the second decade it began to decide larger issues, notably selection of a new site and relocation of the Camp to Painesville in 1924. Other major concerns arose later from the fiscal problems of the depression, staffing of the Camp during the war years, pollution of Lake Erie, and industrialization of the Painesville area.

Starting in the 1950's, the chronicle draws highlights from its other sources, first the development of a professional camping staff and, secondly, the onset of a long search for a new home for JCC's expanding outdoor program. It closes with a series of entries covering the opening of Halle Park in Burton, Ohio, and the last two decades of Camp activity.

Camp Wise today is enriched by its history, but its story, what it was when it started and what it has become, can best be interpreted by a dual theme — Americanization and the Jewish heritage. In its early years and well into the 1920's, Camp Wise centered its efforts on Americanizing an immigrant membership. Later, when an Americanized generation of young people appeared on the scene, it began to adjust its camping program, especially in response to the Jewish Welfare Board survey by Oscar I. Janowsky, published in 1948. The survey's primary recommendation guides the JCC movement to this day — to strengthen its Jewish orientation and take on a deeper distinctive Jewish character. To this changed focus has been added an essential modern Israeli component.

These two elements, Judaism and Israel, weld into the expanding theme of how JCC camping helps young people adjust to being Jewish in an open society. They give the annals of Camp Wise their meaning and significance for our community. Then, as we read and enjoy, we will better understand.

A final word about the dating of entries in the Chronicle. Unless otherwise indicated, entries for the years 1907-1948, are from the minutes book of the Camp Wise Association.

Judah Rubinstein

Camp Wise
Chronicle

October 9, 1907

Proceedings of Incorporators

On the 9th day of October, 1907, Samuel D. Wise, [Rabbi] Moses J. Gries, Meyer Weil, [Dr.] Isadore Grossman, and Eugene L. Geismer, the persons named below as subscribers of articles of incorporation, desiring for themselves, their associates, successors, and assigns to become a body corporate, not for profit in accordance with the general corporation laws of the State of Ohio, under the name and style of the Camp Wise Association, and with all the corporate rights, powers, privileges, and liabilities enjoyed under or imposed by such laws, did subscribe and acknowledge, as required by law, articles of incorporation as follows to wit:

State of Ohio
These Articles of Incorporation of
Camp Wise Association

Witnesseth, That we, the undersigned, all of whom are citizens of the State of Ohio desiring to form a corporation not for profit, under the general corporation laws of said State hereby certify:

First. The name of said corporation shall be The Camp Wise Association.

Second. Said corporation shall be located and its principal business transacted at Cleveland in Cuyahoga County, Ohio.

Third. The purpose for which said corporation is formed is to establish and maintain a fresh air camp for boys and girls and such other persons as may be admitted; to hold real estate and to receive, use, and hold gifts, donations and bequests for the benefit of such corporation, and to do all things necessary and incidental to establish, maintain, and carry on said camp. In Witness Whereof, we have herewith set our hands this 9th day of October, A.D., 1907.

> Samuel D. Wise
> Moses J. Gries
> Meyer Weil
> Isadore Grossman
> Eugene L. Geismer

November 26, 1907

Pursuant to formal notice given to the subscribers of the Articles of Incorporation of the Camp Wise Association and to the members of said association to meet at the Temple, Cleveland, Ohio on the 26th day of November, 1907, at 8 o'clock for the purpose of electing the First Board of Trustees of said corporation, and of transacting such other business as might come before said meeting, the following persons met at the time and place above named: Rabbi Moses J. Gries, Rabbi Louis Wolsey, Mr. Meyer Weil, Isadore Grossman, Mr. Eugene Geismer, Mrs. A. Wiener, Mrs. Louis Grossman. Miss Ida Schott, Miss Beatrice Moss, Miss Lily Sloss, Miss Molly Stearn.

The Chairman declared the election of officers next in order, and nominations having been made and a ballot taken, Mr. Eugene Geismer was duly elected President, Miss Beatrice Moss, Vice President, Miss Molly Stearn, Secretary, and Isadore Grossman, Treasurer.

On motion of Mrs. A. Wiener, duly seconded, it was resolved that the members of the Association call upon Mr. Samuel D. Wise on the afternoon of Thanksgiving Day and thank him in person for his magnificent gift ["the real estate including, buildings, improvements, etc., of every character whatever, of which I am now the present owner, situated at Noble Post Office, Cuyahoga County, on Lake Erie, and formerly known as Stein's on the Lake."]

May 12, 1908

Mr. Edgar Hahn then took an oath faithfully to discharge his duties as a Trustee of the Camp Wise Association.

Mr. [Rabbi] Gries, serving on the special committee on milk, reported that he was making investigations and would report further, at the next meeting.

Mr. Geismer read a list of rules and regulations drawn up by the Executive Committee for those making application to the Camp. After discussion it was voted that these rules be adopted as read and be printed for circulation in Yiddish as well as in English.

June 9, 1908

Mr. Geismer recommended employing Mr. Abel Warschawsky [sic] for the boys. A motion was made by Mrs. Wiener, duly seconded and carried that Mr. W. be employed at a salary of $50.00 a month.

1908
From Notes for A Camp Wise History (1937)

. . . the first group to use this land [in 1908] consisted of 25 boys from C.E.A. and 25 girls from the Council of Jewish Women. This number grew during the summer until there was a total of 100 people at camp during the two-week period. . . After the first two weeks the group not only consisted of boys and girls but of mothers and small children. Because of this variation of age, particularly from six months to 80 years, the program of entertainment was very difficult.

The groups came to camp on Monday for the two-week period. They came out to camp on the Red Interurban, which was the main means of transportation. The children carried their clothes in baskets, since at that time suitcases weren't so common.

When they arrived at camp all the children were washed in Hygieno, their heads were dipped, and they were all sent to the Lake to be washed.

A day at camp consisted of the following: Charley blew the bugle at 6:30 a.m. There were the setting up exercises for boys, followed by the dip. Breakfast at 7:30. Clean-up Squads. There was a flag given at the end of the week to the group which had received the most flags. During the early years the children often received treats from friends who were anxious to do something for the campers. From 9:30-11:30 was the play time period. . . . At 11:30 there was a bathing period with instruction. A lunch then a rest hour followed by a play time and stories and another swim and then supper.

On Monday nights there was usually a bonfire on the beach followed by songs, dramatics, stories. Wednesday night was amateur night, usually in the building. Saturday they had a dance, since a large number of campers consisted of working girls.

During the day there were often short hikes to places near camp occasionally even going to Euclid Creek. Often there were baseball games with the campers from Goodrich Camp which was close by.

August 23, 1908
First Annual Meeting of the Camp Wise Association at the Camp

A motion was made by Mrs. Wiener, duly seconded and carried that a rising note of thanks be given to the young men and women as an expression of appreciation for the splendid work done at the Camp.

September 7, 1908

A motion was made, duly seconded and carried that Charles Dietz be employed at the Camp over the winter at a maximum salary of $12.00 per month.

May 11, 1909

It was moved, seconded, and carried that the Grounds Committee be authorized to buy a horse at a cost not exceeding $50.

June 15, 1909

The Executive Committee reported that Alex Warschawsky [sic] has been employed as boys worker.

September 28, 1909

It was voted that the Board accept with thanks the offer from Mrs. A.E. Brown to build an emergency hospital cottage.

July 12, 1910

It was voted that Charlie Dietz's salary be raised to $60.00 per month and that further arrangements with him be referred to the Executive Committee.

A motion was made by Mrs. Wiener, duly seconded and carried that a letter of thanks be sent to Mrs. Stotter for her gift of a mothers' cottage and dining room and to Mrs. L.J. Grossman for furnishing the social room.

September 27, 1910

A motion was made by Miss Schott, duly seconded and carried that sufficient funds be expended to provide picture postals for the use of the Campers.

June 6, 1911

A motion was made by Mrs. Wiener that the request of the Divinsker [sic] Benevolent Association to hold a picnic at the Camp be refused. The motion was amended by Miss Moses to read that the request be refused if refreshments be for sale, otherwise that the Assoc. be granted permission to hold a picnic at Camp Wise. The amendment was carried.

August 27, 1911
Fourth Annual Meeting of Camp Wise Association at the Camp

A motion was made by Mrs. Hahn, duly seconded and carried that a vote of thanks be extended to the Letter Carriers' band for the splendid music furnished during the afternoon.

June 18, 1913

The beneficiary committee reported the dues were changed to $.75 for children and $1.25 for adults [for a week].

October 30, 1913

It was moved and seconded that the president appoint a committee of five to arrange for the first meeting of a permanent organization of the leaders of Camp Wise.

June 11, 1915

A motion was made by Rabbi Gries, duly seconded and carried that the President be empowered to fill the next vacancy on the Board by Mr. William Treuhaft [elected August 6, 1915, to new post of financial secretary].

It was with extreme regret that the board was forced to accept the resignation of Mr. Geismer, the president. . . . Miss Lily Sloss was unanimously elected president.

August 22, 1915
Eighth Annual Meeting at Camp

No further business, the meeting was adjourned. The guests were then invited to see one of the finest entertainments ever held at Camp Wise —a circus. The ring was held on the grounds, and the sideshows in the Recreation Pavilion.

September 29, 1915

Miss Schott reported for the Beneficiary Committee. The number of applications were three times the number of investigations [carried out]. There were about 3,500 applications. During the past summer there was scarcely a time when there was an empty bed.

December 12, 1916

Upon motion by Mr. Wise and duly seconded, the president with a committee of two was authorized to look into the matter of employing a social worker for next summer. All voted in favor except Mr. Geismer.

April 18, 1917

Miss Schott had accepted the position as social worker and leader at the Camp for the coming season. Miss Schott said that in so doing she expected to bring the camp closer to the Alliance and vice versa.

August 19, 1917
Eleventh Annual Meeting at Camp

Camp accommodated 818 people, 40 more than last summer. About 35,000 meals were served. . . .

September 4, 1917

Miss Schott gave an interesting resume of her work at Camp during the past summer . . . Miss Schott stated how surprisingly much was spent for sweets by the campers who could not afford to pay the fee at Camp.

Upon motion by Mr. [Rabbi] Wolsey and duly seconded, the president was asked to name a committe to prepare a program for religious and moral education at Camp.

An invitation to the installation exercises of Rabbi A. H. Silver was read. The secretary was asked to write the acceptance.

December 4, 1917

Rabbi A.H. Silver was unanimously elected as member of the board to fill the unexpired term of Mr. [Nathan] Loeser.

April 2, 1918

Mr. Treuhaft, expecting to enter the service of the U.S., had to resign his work. It certainly was accepted with deep regret (by the board) as Mr. Treuhaft had been of great service to the board and the Camp.

The fees are to remain as last year. $1.25 per week for adults and $.75 for children, $2.00 for working girls and boys.

April 19, 1918
Report Annual Meeting Camp Wise Association — Ida Schott

Camp Wise is about to close its twelfth season, and in the opinion of many of our campers, it seems to have been the most satisfactory one of all. We have had near record crowds all summer: 296 girls, 272 boys, 75 mothers, and 146 babies; *a total of 789* were accommodated for a period of two weeks. To this large family, we served more than 35,000 meals . . . .

. . . very good wholesome food has been served. Our cook, Mrs. Hollander, and her able assistant, Mrs. Gordon, both of whom are Jewish, have shown a fine spirit in trying to satisfy the appetites of our campers. Our campers frequently say that they taste the Jewish fingers in the food. . . .

We still feel that the system of volunteer leadership as instituted years ago, by those who so wisely planned Camp Wise is good. We have had our full quota of girls leaders . . . . We did not always have enought men leaders, but Mr. Isserman, the director of our boys, succeeded with the aid of a few in giving our boys a splendid time. Our service flag with forty stars tells the story of our absent leaders. The campers miss them and they inquire frequently about them. . . .

May 28, 1918

Miss Schott's report for the Beneficiary committee told of the meetings held with the various investigators and nurses. A few things emphasized at the meeting were:

a. Tuberculosis had increased in the poorer districts and that many were underfed and undernourished . . . .

November 25, 1918

Communications . . . from the Jewish Orphan Asylum thanking the Board of Camp Wise Association . . . for the use of the Camp Grounds for one week after the close of the regular season . . . .

From the resolution of Camp Association Board on death of Rabbi Gries

Rabbi Gries did more than found Camp Wise. He installed in the young people of our community a sense of their responsibility for those less fortunate and developed in them the desire to give [of] themselves in the making of happiness for others and upon these legacies depends the success of the Camp.

March 19, 1919

The election of officers followed:

Mr. William Treuhaft — President
Dr. J. Grossman — Vice President
Tina G. Bernstein — Secretary
S. D. Wise — Treasurer

Mr. S. D. Wise, the treasurer, reported the budget for the ensuing year was about one-third larger than the year previous. The Federation of Jewish Charities had granted the Camp Wise Association $8,000 for the year 1919.

April 16, 1920

Miss Schott reported on her investigations for raising the fees of our campers. The following schedule was accepted:

Children — $1.00 per week
Mothers — $2.00 per week
Working Boys & Girls — $3.00 per week

June 15, 1920

> A motion by Mr. Hahn and duly seconded was to restrict visiting to the Campers on Wednesdays and Sundays, and that only campers be privileged to bathe.

September 10, 1920

> It was moved and seconded to limit visitors to the Camp to Sundays only.

December 17, 1920

> It was moved and seconded that the Secretary write to Mr. Vineberg, the new head of the Alliance, welcoming him to our community and hoping we may have close cooperation between Alliance & the Camp.

July 5, 1921

> The report on the progress of procuring a new Camp Site could not be given at this meeting.

December 18, 1921

> . . . the president was asked to appoint a committee of five to look up new Camp sites and report at the next meeting.

January 26, 1922

> It was decided to place the Camp Wise Property on the market, price suggested $100,000.

June 9, 1922

> Mr. Treuhaft stated that Euclid Village would buy Camp Wise for $95,000.

December 21, 1922

> A motion was made by Mr. Hahn, seconded by Mr. Geismer, to purchase a piece of property from Storrs and Harrison for $75,000.

March 24, 1924

> Miss Schott was asked to see Rabbi [Solomon] Goldman and report on his views of kosherizing [sic] Camp.

April 23, 1924

Miss Schott reported on her interview with Rabbi Goldman, points stressed: (1) Two sets of dishes; (2) Two sets of cooking utensils; (3) Kosher meats.

June 3, 1924

Mr. Treuhaft reported that the Nickel Plate R.R. would furnish free transportation to campers on Tuesday and Wednesday. Taking people out at 8:30 p.m. on Wednesday and the return would be Tuesday noon. It was recommended that the Leaders' Committee arrange to have at least four leaders go out with the children.

Mr. Treuhaft appointed Miss Schott, Miss Printz and Mrs. Wise as a committee to meet with the Federation Kosherizing [sic] Committee.

December 8, 1924

Mr. Treuhaft reported that the Community Fund had given us $14,000 for operating expenses for the coming year; our budget called for $15,208. We received $13,600 last year.

January 12, 1925

Mr. Treuhaft reported . . . Mt. Sinai would not include us in their Campaign, as they will conduct a non-sectarian Campaign and our Camp is known to be distinctly Jewish . . . .

Mrs. Rothenberg made a motion . . . to have Mrs. Hahn write a letter to Mt. Sinai Hospital stating that our Camp is being run as a Health Camp relieving them of a great deal of work and if they received more in their campaign than their goal, to remember us.

August 30, 1925

The Milk Line Group consists of all those boys and girls who were at all underweight, also all children under 5 years, nursing mothers, and special convalescent cases. About 600 individuals received extra milk. These were supplied with milk, or milk and crackers, twice a day at 9:30 a.m. and 2:30 p.m.

1926 Report

Our program this year was perhaps not as standardized as in former years, it being our belief that there is a danger of carrying standardization too far, as it is in many institutions. Camp Wise is not an institution as such. It is rather a place to laugh and sing, to swim and play, to feel happier and stronger, and for two weeks to live in unison with the trees, woods and stars. It should be a place where mothers and children forget their cares and ailments enough to seek new visions and hopes in the wonders of the out-of-doors. In other words, it must be a real Home of Happiness for these two weeks. . . .

August 15, 1926

Mr. Al Brown — head of boys' work — was most enthusiastically received, and from what each worker said of him, he is well deserving of such praise.

January 24, 1927
Minutes of Camp Study Committee of CW Assoc.

After considerable discussion, the committee finally voted the following recommendation:

That in the future, Camp Wise give equal recognition to nutrition cases and environmentally underprivileged children, in addition, admitting those who possess physical defects that might be improved by a stay at camp but that do not materially interfere or are not especially detrimental to the carrying out of the program with the nutrition and environmentally underprivileged children.

April 3, 1928

A motion was made by Mrs. Rothenberg and seconded by Dr. Markey to approve the following scale of fees for 1928:

Children under 3 years	$ 1.00 per trip
" 3-5 years inclusive	3.00 per trip
" 6-12 years inclusive	4.00 per trip
" 13-16 years and over	6.00 per trip
Mothers	7.00 per trip
Working boys and girls	10.00 per trip

May 21, 1928

Mr. Grossman suggested the following resolution be put on file and sent to the Bureau of Jewish Education. It was accepted by the Board.

RESOLVED: That it is the sense of the Board of the Camp Wise Association to devote part of the time of the Camp program in fostering Jewish education and ideals, and that The Camp Wise Association is in sympathy and would like to assist in carrying out a program that the Bureau would suggest.

September 11, 1928

Miss Schott expressed the regret of the members of the board at Mr. Treuhaft's leaving the presidency, after so many years of untiring service.

July 28, 1929

. . . it was felt Camp was serving the needs of a different class of people than heretofore. The number of children coming from the 55th and Woodland district and the J.S.S.B. [Jewish Social Service Bureau] . . . and other such organizations is comparatively smaller than in previous years, due no doubt to restricted immigration.

October 5, 1929

Miss Schott reported on the Campers during the past session. It was almost impossible to fill camp with the class we have had in years gone by. Economic conditions and lack of immigration brought about the change.

April 6, 1930

The following resolution was made by Mr. Treuhaft and duly seconded. Resolved that there be the closest cooperation between the recruiting forces of the Alliance and Camp Wise toward the elimination of competition between the two institutions for campers [Camp Wise and CEA Camp Henry Baker] . . . .

August 20, 1931
The Gong — The First Alliwise

The one thing that makes us wish we were older, and we're getting along nicely, thank, you, is the wish that we might have been numbered among those who attended Alliwise at its initial opening. Back in 1916 — the heavy, black war clouds of the world hanging low and ready to burst with its ruinous deluge.

Yet a group of young men, some who might be called in their country's service, centered around Mr. Solomon and Miss Schott and spent a week at Alliwise, free from cares and worries of these troubled days.

We can not think of them all, and those whose names are omitted are requested to submit them so that this truly roll of honor may be preserved for all time. These were Leo Ascherman, Dan Wasserman, Harry Lipson, Sidney Katzman, Eli Drucker, Aaron Goldman, Hy Gittleson, Jack Gittleson, Sam Brown, Sam Rose and Charles Shaffer.

November 8, 1931
The Gong — Purely Personal Piffle

Very few old timers were out at Camp this year; but a few came out for that Sunday ballgame, among whom were Harry Blachman, Mickey Danaceau, Ezra Shapiro and Aaron Goldman.

July 8, 1932

The director, Mr. Kinoy, when introduced said he thought it a privilege to be back in Cleveland and at Camp Wise. His aim was to have a happy camp —where campers and leaders would feel a real intimacy.

December 5, 1932

A letter from the Federation announced more drastic cuts. The Budget Committee was asked to meet and consider the necessary reductions to meet the budget.

June 10, 1933
The Gong— From letter by Si Posner, now in New York

Alliwise brings to mind memories — but the memories are not ones of any particular incidents, but rather a recollection of the friendly spirit that prevails.

I cannot help but think that 16-18 years ago, when problems of home or school perplexed us and we would wander into the office of Mr. Solomon. In this room we unburdened our hearts and our minds and received comfort and help to the many problems of adolescence. His influence, help and guidance will never be forgotten by many of us.

August 1, 1933
The Gong

Al Brown and Co. have opened their Camp Caravan. A good emblem for Al's Camp would be a camel, we think . . . . And Mrs. Al has a camp for little girls which we think is so nice because when the boys of Al's camp grow up and are old enought to swear and have their own first door key, they can truthfully say: "We went to different camps together."

June 12, 1935

Chairman of Budget, Mr. Treuhaft, reported a total of $10,750 had been allocated to Camp for 1935.

May 1, 1936
Gong Portrait — Jac Fallenberg

Jac was a member of the Old Beam Club. Leave the "k" off his name so you'll remember him. . . . Is a voracious reader but will leave off anything to eat . . . Practices law when he isn't saving some business or other, specializes in leases . . . Has a devastating sense of humor. Either you laugh or you're devastated . . . A scientist, therapist, idealist and conversationalist, yet withal, a human being . . . Originated the word "cliffing" at Alliwise. Can't swim a stroke but takes a bath alone . . . Spent hours working on a pun but honest enough to feel sorry after he's made it.

June 3, 1936
Executive Meeting of the Crew Board and Association Board.

Mr. Rose, President of the Crew, explained that the policy of the Crew has changed. Its chief function is that of training leaders and interesting leaders in the continuation and growth of camp leadership. The Crew recognizing the need for trained leaders held a winter Training Course for eight consecutive weeks. The number of people trained totaled 125. A check-up showed very regular attendance by members, proving interest.

August 30, 1936
30th Anniversary of Camp Wise

Miss Schott expressed the feeling of satisfaction on the fine development of camps today. She told of a visit to Camp Artec in Russia with its excellent equipment and leadership.

July 1, 1937

Mr. Treuhaft suggested the arrangement in the near future of a meeting with the Camp Council to discuss the question of Volunteer Leadership in camping.

October 6, 1938
Letter from Mr. Hiram S. Rivitz, President, Industrial Rayon Corporation

> Mr. George B. Mayer:
>
> I appreciated the opportunity of discussing with you and your associates
> . . . the problems confronting your enterprise [Camp Wise]. . . .
>
> The reactions of the community [Painesville], . . . on the contrary,
> insofar as I have been able to learn is not only favorable toward the
> erection of our plant but I might say enthusiastic for the very good reason
> that it will provide work for hundreds of people who need jobs in that
> community.
>
> I sincerely regret, of course, that Camp Wise happens to be in close
> proximity to our plant . . . .
>
> The location of Camp Wise was probably all right in its day, but coming
> down to brass tacks, I am sure that you would not say your facilities for
> bathing, your drinking water and your sanitation have been ideal or all
> that could be wished for. Of course you did the best you could with what
> you had, and I can understand the merit of a desire . . . to move the
> Camp to some spot in the interior where you would have more modern
> facilities; but this desire, I am sure, was not prompted entirely by the fact
> that we happened to have built a plant near the Camp.
>
> I think you know that I am always ready to do what I can for the very
> worthwhile service you and your associates are rendering to the community
> . . . but in this era in which we are living, progress in industry is of vital
> importance to the welfare of any community, and there is not a community
> in the United States that would not jump at the chance to locate a plant
> such as ours in their midst regardless of other considerations. The
> payment of taxes by our company, payrolls, general business acceleration
> in the community, the building of homes, are only possible through
> payrolls.

July 29, 1941
Camp Wise Executive Board Meeting

> Mr. Kinoy reported on Camp for the season of 1941 up to date.
> Everything is in excellent condition and running smoothly. There is some
> trouble in getting leaders. The problem of transportation to Painesville
> and Greenwald's farm was discussed. Mr. Kinoy reported that the Camp

car was in very poor condition. It was moved and seconded that taxis be used to transport children the remainder of the season.

February 17, 1942

Mr. [George] Hays read a letter from Mr. Kinoy. The letter stated that because of war, school teachers in New York State were being asked to work this summer and that under the circumstances he would be unable to work this summer. Mr. Hays said that the position had been offered to Sidney Vincent on a permanent basis. A letter from Mr. Vincent was read giving his reasons for not being able to accept the position.

. . . The subject of war protection, blackouts, etc., was brought up by Mr. Hays. Mr. Halle suggested fire drills. It was also moved and seconded that advice on air raid precautions be asked for from Camp Council.

June 30, 1942

It was reported that children over 16 were also difficult to handle this year because of the youth of the councilors.

February 1, 1943
Statement Regarding the Merger of Camp Wise and Camp Henry Baker

The Boards of Trustees of the Camp Wise Association and of the Council Educational Alliance have considered it advisable to integrate the services of Camp Wise and Camp Henry Baker through experimental merger of the camps.

In this new arrangment, much becomes effective immediately, both units will be operated as one camp to be known as Camp Wise. The camp will have a single staff and program, as well as a unified intake. The Camp Wise Assocation will be responsible for the work of the merged camps and the Council Educational Alliance will be represented on the board of the Camp Wise Association. Camp Henry Baker will hereafter be designated as the Henry Baker Buildings of Camp Wise.

The plan provides that the administration of Camp Wise be vested in the executive director of the Council Educational Alliance, who shall be responsible to the board of the Camp Wise Association with respect to the work of the camp.

August 4, 1943

Howard Robbins reported on the farm program. He said that the farm children were working very industriously and that the project was quite successful. The program may be extended week-ends after camp closes if the farmers need the extra help.

Sidney Vincent reported on Camp. His report mentioned difficulties in the kitchen — difficulties in obtaining meat — the immaturity of the councilors.

November 24, 1943

The President stated that the meeting had been called to consider the following matter. Approximately two weeks before, the Industrial Rayon Corporation had requested permission to use the Camp's facilities during the winter and spring of 1943 and 1944, for the purpose of housing laborers needed in the construction of an addition to the Industrial Rayon Corporation plant. This addition is to be built to provide facilities for immediately essential War production. . . . The Committee agreed to permit Industrial Rayon Corporation to use the Camp facilities for this purpose on the Corporation's agreement that it would winterize the buildings at its own expense, that it would restore the buildings to their present good condition before the 1944 camp season, that it would surrender the facilties to the Camp before June 1, 1944, in complete good use for summer camp use . . . and that it would donate $5,000 to the Camp Wise Association. In the interests of the war effort, Henry Zucker moved that the Board members endorse the agreement, seconded by Bill Treuhaft. Motion carried.

December 14, 1943

Be it further resolved that the action of the Board of Trustees taken at its special meeting on the 24th day of November, 1943, authorizing the giving of permission to Industrial Rayon Corporation to use the Camp Wise premises and facilities be, and the same is hereby satisfied and confirmed.

. . . After discussion the resolution was unanimously adopted.

April 14, 1944

On motion duly made, seconded and unanimously adopted, the Committee recommended to the Camp Wise Association Board that joint operation of Camp Wise and Camp Henry Baker be continued for another year. In discussion of this motion, the opinion was expressed that a joint Camp Wise Board-Council Educational Alliance Board committee begin investigation of a means of effecting a permanent consolidation operation.

April 18, 1944

Sanford Solender then reported on a "Plan for Extension of Case Work Consultation Service To Camp Wise [with Jewish Family Service Association case workers]." William Treuhaft moved that the report and its plan be adopted as presented. The motion was seconded and unanimously carried.

Howard Robbins, leader of the farm group last year and again for the coming season, reported that while more work commitments were already obtained than had been obtained in advance last year, the search for employment will still be a major problem this summer. Last year the farmers paid 35 cents per hour for inexperienced help and 40 cents for experienced workers; 40 and 45 cents respectively will be asked this year. The berry picking price will depend on the market for berries.

June 7, 1944

The Secretary read a letter sent by Leon Weil, as President of the Camp Wise Association Board, to the Industrial Rayon Corporation, acknowledging return of the Camp property in satisfactory condition. . . . Hiram Rivitz, President of Rayon Corporation, was complimented for the manner in which camp property was cared for during occupancy.

Hugo Mahrer reported on improvements that had been made to the Camp property by Industrial Rayon Corporation. Each cottage now had a shower room. Special shower rooms were built as additions to the boys' and girls' cottages and, in the former mothers' cottages. The old kitchens were made into shower rooms. The plumbing throughout had been winterized. The walks had been graveled; . . . a new concrete floor installed in the basement under the kitchen, and many other important and smaller items have been added.

Sanford Solender reported respecting the staff situation. . . . A few vacancies still remained to be filled. He also reported that the Federal Farm Subsidy would be renewed this year and that Camp Wise has been certified for the Camp Lunch Program and will receive nine cents [per camper] per day to enrich the regular diet.

November 14, 1944

Report presented by Mr. Solender on subject "Does the higher economic status of our clientele mean that Camp is not serving the proper people in the community?" Mr. Solender stated that an investigation of the records of 100 of our families has shown:

1. Camp is serving the same group it always has served.

2. The capacity of these people to pay higher fees has increased greatly.

3. We are drawing our campers from the same residential areas as in recent years.

January 9, 1945

The chairman . . . indicated that negotiations had been taking place relative to the use of camp by the [Industrial Rayon] Corporation during the winter months for the housing of Japanese-American workers.

March 27, 1945

. . . that the Board approve a Youth Camp for 14-16 year olds as outlined in the Committee Report [Committee on Camping for Adolescents], the said Camp to be an integral part of Camp Wise; that emphasis be on a Work Program, whether Crop or In-Camp Work Projects, with a carefully supervised Recreation program for the group. The motion was carried.

June 8, 1945

A letter from the Orthodox Committee expressed great satisfaction with the changes made in the commissary to conform with their wishes and with our agreement to make the Camps strictly kosher.

November 19, 1946

Most of the evening was devoted to discussion of the new Agreement for the operation of Camp Wise by the C.E.A. . . . It was moved by Mr. Treuhaft and seconded by Mr. Mahrer that this report and agreement be accepted. Motion was passed.

1946 Program Report — Camp Wise Program Director, Bernice Teitelbaum

In reviewing the work of Camp Wise for 1946 we are gratified at the extent to which we were able at many points to come closer to attaining our objectives. We recognize that providing campers with two or three weeks of happy, healthy outdoor living is an important part of our job, but even more so is the realization that what we hope to do is expose the children to the kind of experience in group living which will have some carry-over after they have left the camp setting.

. . . Education along lines of interracial understanding and questions of significance has long been a concern of the Camp Wise staff. Most of the important work along this line was done from day to day in the living group through discussions and through projects which centered on cultural groups. . . .

September 29, 1948
Minutes, Jewish Welfare Federation Board of Trustees

The Secretary reported that the Jewish Community Center is ready to start its operations on October 1st. The Board is asked to approve the transfer to the JCC of the allocations previously approved through December 31, 1948, for the Jewish Young Adult Bureau, the Cultural Department of the Jewish Community Council, and the Council Educational Alliance.

February 1955
Camp Wise Notes — WHAT IS "JEWISH LIVING" AT CAMP?

Jewish life consists of: (1) a set of values which direct our actions. (2) a variety of traditions and practices handed down by our ancestors. (3) a history of the achievements of the Jewish people and (4) music, dancing and other activities which are an expression of the feelings of our people. We feel an obligation at camp to include a good sampling of all these as part of daily living.

November 20, 1957
Opening Remarks by President of JCC, Morton Mandel, at JCC Ninth Annual Meeting re Camp Wise Fiftieth Anniversary

Let us review in our minds the procession over these fifty years of the thousands upon thousands of boys and girls, mothers and young ones who found at Camp Wise a period of relaxation, of good fellowship and of education in the outdoors, in the beautiful natural surroundings of our camp — first the old at Euclid, Ohio and than this camp which was built a generation ago. Think of the good times and the solid friendships camp provided. Think of the leadership training that hundreds of our young men and women gained here. Think of the many happy marriages which grew out of acquaintance made at camp. Think of the service given to our country in two world wars by both campers and leaders, and the service given by our campers and leaders to our own community over the half century.

1957 Season — Camp Wise Report to JCC Board of Trustees
Abe Bonder, Director

It is this camp director's unique situation to be able to look back personally over almost half of the camp's existence . . . I recall the earnest meetings our key staff held during the spring of 1935, the meticulous preparation for the Spring Institute, the careful outlining of program and procedures. I have yet to find a more tireless combination of co-workers than Dorothy Wahl, Ruth Kline, Dave Hilberman, and Al Friedman. I must admit that I learned far more from them in 1935 than I was able to contribute. Being then somewhat a novice at administrative responsibility I was a clumsy worker by comparison, but that season opened my eyes to many important aspects of camping.

As I look back, I am today amazed at the creative skills and the energy shown by these workers and by my co-worker, Sid Vincent, who was then also new to this activity. The manner in which they were able to cram into a scant two weeks a procession of day-by-day activities — crafts, nature lore, games, music, swimming, campcraft, and others and then to top off most evenings with a spectacular evening theme program in which almost every person in camp was a participant, most often in costume and makeup, was phenomenal. The color and spirit of those evenings has remained in my memory over all these years.

The functioning of the Camp Wise Crew at that time was also a great inspiration. It was stirring to see this group of young people, a cross-section of the social and economic community, banded together to help in the provision of a summer camping experience for the children of our city. This, at least, seemed to be one of the more constructive features of life during the depression. . . .

Probably the major advance over our past generation of work with children has been the developing understanding of the needs of children and the development of more constructive ways of working with them. I am only too conscious now of the extremes we have used. I remember how we greeted our campers as they arrived in 1935 by lining them up and deliberately separating one friend from another to "avoid cliques" and the "resultant troublemaking." We did not yet understand that children in a strange place need to be made to feel at home and that established friendships provide a feeling of security which can be expanded in the daily living at camp as children make new friends. While we still have not entirely succeeded in dealing with this, we have achieved many fine results in helping campers learn to get along with new people and to accept differences among people. . . .

I feel that a sign of growing maturity has been the movement toward a balance in our outlook. We want campers to learn to help plan and create program. We want them to learn how to work together and how to accept responsibility. We want to provide opportunity for them to try out ideas and to learn from trial and error. However, we must teach them the basic skills and knowledge upon which to build. We start with the youngest —

our eight year olds — by making various program plans for them but then giving them some freedom of choice in activities . . . When they reach the age of about twelve years, we help them organize an elected council which will meet with staff to make plans. However, we assume that the obligation of the adult leaders is to set up the range of activities within realistic limits of our time, facilities and resources.

We constantly encourage interest in activities which we feel are particularly appropriate to camp. We urge campcraft, nature lore, hiking and campfires instead of baseball and basketball (which we allow some time for on a voluntary basis). Instead of jitterbugging, we teach the folk dances of many lands including the Israeli. Instead of the usual popular songs, we present varied folk songs. As the camp of the Jewish community, we automatically observe Jewish occasion, including the Sabbath, but we also involve the campers in varying degrees according to their abilities in the preparation of services and other activities related to the occasions . . . .

1959 Season — Camp Wise Report

The weather was the best for summer camping we have had for the past four years. The weather was usually warm and rainy days were quite scattered . . . .

However, the level of the water in the lake was lower than I have seen it in the past eight years. Therefore, our beach was almost non-existent and swimming conditions were, to say the least, exceedingly poor . . . .

The general reaction of the campers seemed very good. The relationship between campers and counselors was for the most part excellent . . . .

This summer served to point out most dramatically the unfortunate situation of the present camp site. The season opened with a hot spell and one of our immediate concerns became that of overexposure of campers to too much sun. Every elm tree on the main area of the camp has now been destroyed by the elm blight, and we were often forced to keep the children indoors part of the day in order to make sure that they were not over-exposed to sunburn.

December 24, 1962
Minutes of Camp Committee Meeting

The committee concluded that the Friends of Camp site near Burton, Ohio, is the best which has been located this far and should be accepted as the site for the development of a new camp . . . . This recommendation was accepted by the Board of Trustees [JCC] on October 24, 1962.

February 1963
Letter from JCC (Ernest H. Siegler, President, and Arthur H. Dettelbach, Chairman, Camp Development Committee, to Harold Galvin, Chairman, Social Agency Committee, J.C.F.)

The community has been aware for many years of the inadequacies of the present Camp Wise location . . . .

In 1953, at the request of the Jewish Community Federation, an outline of the requirements for a new resident camp facility was drawn up by our Camp Committee . . . .

During the next five years, the Camp Committee made a wide search for a new site. . . . As a result of that search, a fine potential site of 325 acres near Burton, Ohio, was located in 1958. This site was purchased by a group of Friends of Camp [cost approximately $70,000] and has been held for possible resale, at cost, to the Jewish community to serve as the new location for our camp. This arrangement was reported in detail to the Jewish Community Federation and the Social Agency Committee in 1958. The voting trust arrangement on the prospective site specifies that it must be purchased by the Jewish Community Center by November 1, 1963. In June, 1963, we will therefore formally request permission from the Social Agency Committee to purchase this site.

. . . In planning for a solution to some of the basic problems of our camps, it became evident that a very promising plan to accommodate a variety of camping services could be worked out on the one plot of land. On October 24, 1962, the Board of Trustees of the Jewish Community Center adopted the recommendations of the New Camp Development Committee . . . to proceed with all necessary steps to relocate the camping programs on this new site.

. . . The realization of this plan now becomes a necessity because the present Camp Wise site was sold to the Cleveland Electric Illuminating Company in 1960. The proceeds of the sale will be sufficient to meet a major share of a new camp. There is, however, a time limit to our occupancy of present camp. We must give it up at the close of the 1965 season. It is, therefore, urgent that we move forward promptly with the acquisition of the new site and construction of the new camp. . . .

June 19, 1966
Halle Park Dedication Ceremonies — Tablet Text

The Eugene S. and Blanche R. Halle Park
of the Jewish Community Center of Cleveland

These acres of rolling hills and peaceful valleys, lavishly endowed with Nature's most gracious favors, will become a memorial in perpetuity to Eugene and Blanche Halle. These lands will forever be used to afford wholesome recreation and to build health and strength for young and old alike.

This park was made possible to a large extent through a generous gift from the Eugene S. Halle and Blanche R. Halle Memorial Fund of the Cleveland Foundation. Throughout their lives the principal interests of Eugene and Blanche Halle were centered in service to their fellowmen and to institutions which serve them. They saw to it that many vital and worthwhile causes would continue to benefit from their generosity after they passed on. They were unpretentious leaders, dedicated to wholesome and forward-looking living.

Far more precious than their philanthropies was the esteem in which they were held by their fellow-citizens; no two people have ever been held in higher esteem by their community. Every institution which bears their name gains added prestige and strength by reason of the use of their name.

Thus, Halle Park is not only a vital facility for the use of the community, but a symbol of character, a lofty and significant reminder that a good name is our greatest heritage.

August 28, 1966
Halle Park Fact Sheet

. . . . As the project developed it became obvious that additional funds would be needed. Through the Eugene S. and Blanche R. Halle Fund, the Center received a grant of $300,000. This together with the funds realized from the sale of old Camp Wise, made possible the construction of the new Camp. Because it was recognized that several types of outdoor programs would be conducted at this site, the Board of Trustees of the Jewish Community Center designated the overall property as the

EUGENE S. AND BLANCHE R. HALLE PARK

In 1966, the John W. Anisfield Fund of the Cleveland Jewish Community Federation, which has been realized from the sale of old Camp Anisfield, was granted to the Jewish Community Center to help finance the new Day Camp Construction. In recognition of this, the Day Camp is known as the ANISFIELD DAY CAMP. The resident camp returned the name with which it has long been associated — CAMP WISE.

January 11, 1968
Minutes of Halle Park Committee

Mr. Bonder reported that during the summer a team from the Standards Committee of the American Camping Association had visited the camp to check on its compliance with the present standards of the Association. . . .

The report which was received stated: "Lake Erie Section Camp Standards Committee of the A.C.A. is happy to report the camp has been fully accredited. The highest scoring received by your camp was in the area of program, although all areas rated fairly well above the minimum required."

September 1971
Letter from Shaliach [emissary] Ephraim Katz on return home to Haifa, Israel

Thanks to All of You!

All my life I lived in Israel, the place where I was born to my mother, 6th generation Sabra, and my father.

It is my first time leaving Israel and going abroad visiting another country.

I had landed at Cleveland's airport on the 22nd of June and came incidentally to Camp Wise to be a counselor in the Pioneers Village in the Kfar Ivri program.

The two days I spent on my journey were not enough time to have an impression about the people here in the U.S.A.

During my work with the kids first at Pioneer Village then Trailblazers and at last Teen Camp, I realized that things like food, buildings, streets, cars, etc. might be different but kids are all over the world the same and they are sweet and nice just like as they are in Israel.

. . . . Many times while talking and telling about Israel I had this feeling of belonging to the great United Jewish Family even though I didn't know these people before and it might be that I will never see them again. Suddenly, the fact of being a Jew is meaningful so much more than it was when I was in Israel. Now, I know I have a big, friendly family.

I want all of you to feel free to write to me to Israel.

1979
Proposal for the Development of the Leon G. Weil Nature Trail at Camp Wise.

. . . The Nature Trail will be dedicated to the memory of Leon G. Weil, who contributed greatly to Cleveland's Jewish community throughout his adult life. The trail will be constructed at the Jewish Community Center's Camp Wise, where Mr. Weil was a driving force for many years. *RATIONALE:* Leon G. Weil was a lover of both children and the out-of-doors. Camp Wise sees the outdoor experience as an important part of a child's growth and development. It serves to illustrate both the beauty and importance of our natural world, and to enhance appreciation for the relationship between man and his natural environment. A nature trail at Camp Wise will add to and strengthen the out-of-door experience for all the children who attend camp for years to come. A permanent nature trail will also greatly broaden the present Outdoor Education program of the camp.

November 30, 1983
Minutes, JCC Board of Trustees

The Jewish program again was a major strength. The Jewish Welfare Board has indicated that Camp Wise is a national model camp in terms of its Jewish programming.

POSTSCRIPT

Camp Wise is a story of its own, of people and places. In this chronicle covering 80 years, we read of its establishment and changing geography, its years of program trial and adjustment, its staff professionalization, and its placement in time as a cornerstone of Cleveland Jewish life. Three final observations capture the essence of these principal topics and summarize this brief chronicle.

The first is excerpted from an appreciation by Matt Elson, who went on from Cleveland and Camp Wise to become a social worker, later a staff member of the National Jewish Welfare Board, and finally, for the major part of his professional career, executive director of the New Jersey YM-YWHA Camps. As he recalls, it all began for him at age seven with a single two-week trip to the first Camp Wise in Euclid, Ohio, and later in 1931 as a teenage volunteer counselor at the Painesville site.

Camp Wise was a very happy and rewarding experience. The kids were fun and lovable, and the counselor staff was made up of very special people — I found a happy home . . . .

In my career as a social worker . . . I never forgot, or ceased to marvel in memory, at the quality of service to children that was achieved at this particular time and place by short-term volunteers.

I returned to Camp Wise for a couple of college summers, but was then recruited . . . for Camp Baker across the ravine. And it was this combination of experiences which drew me into social work training, a return to the CEA as a branch director and to Camp Baker as its director, settlement and Jewish Center work. . . .

And it all started a million years ago — with two weeks at the place called Camp Wise.

The second by Dave Apple, associated with Camp Wise for 60 years, represents the community's support and commitment to camping as part of its system of services. He started out at Camp Wise in 1929 as a staff member and went on to serve to this day on committees, often chaired by him, that helped guide and oversee its present complex operation.

In our ever-changing world, one constant stable feature at Camp Wise has been our emphasis on providing a good camping environment for these children attending our Camp. The camp activities were aimed at helping children in their social adjustment, strengthening their Jewish identity, and acquainting them with their natural environment.

With the growth in expertise of our professional staff, we have expanded our program. . . . The event of the establishment of the State of Israel has enormously enriched programs involving dramatics, handicrafts, singing, and the speaking of Hebrew language, all working toward strengthening our Jewish identity.

Camp Wise continues to meet the needs of our Jewish youth. . . . It is a service we are proud to offer.

The last comment belongs to Al Brown, as valid and warm today as it was in his 1926 report:

Camp Wise is not an institution. It is rather a place to laugh and sing, to swim and play, to feel happier and stronger, and for two weeks to live in unison with the trees and woods and stars. It should be a place . . . to see new visions and hopes in the wonders of the out-of-doors.

The songs of Camp Wise, just like its programs, have changed over time. Parodies, followed by Gilbert and Sullivan songs, followed by hit tunes from Broadway musicals, and now the songs from Israel form the Camp Wise musical heritage and library. This brief account of the origin, development, and changes in the sounds of Camp Wise embellish its record and add a pleasant note to this volume.

In the camp's first four decades, the many parodies were written to well-known American folk tunes, like "Clementine," which the young people easily learned and remembered. Some of these parodies, written by Al Brown, are included in this section also written by him. Others appear as well in Camp song books published in later years. But one of the very popular fun songs to this day, "I Was Born Ten Thousand Years Ago," was introduced seventy years ago by Dr. Oscar Markey, who came here from Pittsburgh in 1919, while still in college, to be head leader of the boys and then camp director for the 1920 and 1921 seasons. He recalls how much he enjoyed leading group singing. This long-time favorite and others make up the repertoire he assembled during his camping experiences.

Songs quickly united campers in bonds of friendship and common experiences on the hiking trail and around the campfire. These songs later set the mood for reunions and reawakened memories of companions and shared days at camp. So, hum along as you read this closing section of The Camp Wise Story.

Camp Wise
Songs

Albert M. Brown

Many years ago, I heard Harry Lauder, that genial Scotsman, come out in front of the curtain at the old Hippodrome, and sing:

> *It's a fine thing to sing,*
> *   Singing is the thing;*
> *It brightens everything*
> *   that may seem dreary;*
>
> *It keeps you on the road,*
> *   When you've got a heavy load,*
> *Yes, singing is the thing*
> *   that makes life cheery!*

Singing has always played an important part in camp. We sing for many reasons and on many occasions: friendship, patriotism, religious songs, and songs for joyous moments and for quieter moods. In camp, singing should be for sheer *fun*! That is how the singing of camp songs began at Camp Wise; for fun and laughter, on the trail, around a campfire, in small groups under a tree, and in those less active periods as the day ended. As with all other programs, there have been noticeable changes in songs at Camp Wise.

In the earlier years, in addition to American folk songs, such as "Clementine" and "I've Been Working on the Railroad" there were mostly "songs of the absurd" for lack of a more descriptive phrase. At that time, these songs were popular, and the campers responded lustily and happily, among them "John Brown's Baby Had A Cold Upon His Chest," with appropriate motions as each word was eliminated; and a song, "O! Mr. Noah, He Built an Ark, Hurrah, Hurrah" to the tune of "When Johnny Comes Marching Home Again;" "Under the Spreading Chestnut Tree;" and the catchy but difficult song that began, "A tree in the woods, the woods in the ground, and the green grass grew all around, all around."

There were many fun songs that had no connection whatsoever with camp life, but for some reason the campers, led by the song leader, relished hearing them and learned every one of these songs before the season ended. The songs included "Little Tom Tinker Was Burnt by a Clinker," "Three Men Went A-Hunting," "Little Sir Echo," "My Name Is Goity Moiphy," and "My Name is Yon Yonson, I Come From Visconsin."

The best example of the absurd and fun type of song, and perhaps the most popular ever sung in the 20's, was introduced by Oscar Markey in 1919, "I Was Born Ten Thousand Years Ago." Sung in limerick style, it was and still is a hit and an ice-breaker for those who hear it for the first time. An audience of children, adults too, can easily and quickly participate. The last two or three words italicized in the following two sample verses are the words repeated by the audience, making it sound like an echo:

Oh, I was born ten thousand years ago (*years ago!*)
   And there isn't anything that I don't know (*I don't know!*)
I was floating down the bay,
   With Methuselah one day,
And I dare you to tell me it isn't so . . . (*it isn't so!*)

I taught Columbus how to find his famous lands (*famous lands*)
   To the Sahara Desert I brought all the sands (*all the sands*)
And for Pharaoh and the kids,
   Why, I built the pyramids,
I taught Samson how to use his mighty hands (*mighty hands!*)

There were a dozen or so verses to begin with, and as certain historical events and important personalities emerged upon the scene, they became subjects for more verses to be written. I still use this song at song-fests with adults, and it never fails to evoke enthusiastic response.

Then came the era of parodies of popular songs to fit the camp atmosphere. The young campers, many of them already familiar with the tunes, quickly learned the easy Wise verses, which added to the spirit of their vacation. In the waking hours campers were roused by this parody of "Roaming in the Gloaming":

Yawning in the morning
   When the breakfast bell we hear,

Yawning in the morning
  When our sleep is very dear;
And when we're fully dressed
  And we think we look the best,
Still we go on
  YAWNING IN THE MORNING

Equally if not more familiar, "In the Good Old Summer Time" was ideal for the House of Happiness:

In the good old camping time,
  In the good old camping time,
Living 'mid the woods and streams,
  What a joy divine!
So give a cheer for our Camp Wise,
  Let its fame reach every clime,
For that's the Home of Happiness
  In the good old camping time.

Hiking songs were special favorites on the outdoor trails. "When the Red, Red Robin Comes Bob, Bob, Bobbin' Along" was the inspiration for a longer verse to cheer the hikers:

When the camp, camp, campers come
  tramp, tramp, trampin' along, along;
Then the air'll be ringing when we start singing
  that old sweet song;
March on, march on, you campers true,
  Look up, look up, the skies are blue,
Watch for, watch for the rainbow's hue,
  March, sing, laugh and be happy;
Storms may threaten us,
  They won't frighten us, after all,
Rains may glisten, but still we'll listen
  For that sweet call;
We are a jolly band, marching hand in hand,
  singing this song,
When the camp, camp, campers
  come tramp, tramp, trampin' along!

Time on the trail allowed campers to learn one of the best hiking songs, written to the tune of the "Light Cavalry Overture":

O! this is the day it is up and away,
  At the peep of early morning,

With staff in hand, an eager band,
  Our hearts as light as air;
In the drum and fife, there is joy in life
  As the earth our feet are scorning,
And off we start, with buoyant heart
  And never a thought of care.
Through the valley low, at our ease we go,
  To the tune the brook is singing,
We mount the hill, with sturdy will
  And spirits ever high;
For the goal's in sight, and we know the night
  To the hardy band is bringing
Inviting beds, for weary heads,
  At the Inn of the Starry Sky . . .

Still another excellent hiking song was one to the tune of "And the Caissons Go Rolling Along":

Over hill, over dale, as we hit the dusty trail,
  And the hikers go marching along;
Voices ring, as we sing, high or low or anything,
  As the hikers go marching along;
For it's hike, hike, hike, on pavement or on pike,
  Step out, with arms a-swinging free,
For night and day, we are on our way,
  As the voice of the road calls to me:
KEEP ON HIKING!
  As the voice of the road calls to me . . .

The campfire was the site for evening programs, often featuring stories, performances by cabin teams, and the spirited parodies with familiar tunes and easily learned verses. "The Old Gray Mare, She Ain't What She Used To Be" became the basis for a repeated three line stanza:

Here we sit like
  Birds in the wilderness (3),
Here we sit like
  Birds in the wilderness,
Waiting for the show to start (3);
Here we sit like
  Birds in the wilderness
Waiting for the show to start.

Borrowing the "Ohio State Fight Song," familiar at least to the boys, made an enthusiastic start to camping:

We welcome you to our Camp Wise,
  We're mighty glad you're here,
We'll send the air reverberating
  With a mighty cheer, Rah! Rah!

We'll sing you in,
  We'll sing you out,
Join us and we'll all give a shout;
  Hail, hail, the gang's all here,
With a welcome to our Camp Wise!

If some parodies were simple and easily memorized, others had longer verses, which required the aid of song sheets. In the closing days of a camping session, some songs began to focus on fixing memories of friends and Camp Wise. For example, "Smile the While, 'Till We Meet Again":

'Round the campfire, 'neath the stars so bright,
  We have met in comradeship tonight;
'Round about these whispering trees,
  Guard our golden memories;
And so before we close our eyes in sleep,
  Let us pledge each other that we'll keep
Camp Wise friendships strong and deep,
  'TILL WE MEET AGAIN.

Other songs to keep yesterday alive were more direct. "Remembering" was straight to the point:

Remember the times we've had here,
  Remember our pleasant stay,
Remember the hikes and swimming
  And don't forget to come back some day;
The campfires and the dramatics,
  The baseball, and friends so true,
O! Camp Wise deserves your friendship,
  Be sure and remember it, too.

During the next several decades, the old songs of the early years were practically set aside, or perhaps not known to new directors and song leaders. There was a gradual change to Gilbert and Sullivan songs, such as "I Am the Captain of the Pinafore" and "We Sail the Ocean Blue"; to songs from musicals of the day, such as "O! What A Beautiful Morning" from "Oklahoma," "Getting to Know You" from "Sound of Music," "Consider Yourself At Home" from "Oliver," and to world peace songs, for example "Let There Be Peace On Earth." These became the new songs of camp.

Then came the most dramatic change in camp songs. In 1948, when the State of Israel was established, every Jewish camp in the country caught the spirit of passionate Jewish commitment in programming and in songs. Israeli songs and dances became an integral part of Camp Wise seasons, and this spirit took over and permeated the programs and group activities. The parents and the children loved this new concept as much as families of the first four decades were fond of their activities and camp songs.

Thus, it was inevitable that the change in camp songs should coincide with all the changes that have taken place in our lives and in the world from the year 1907 to this day and age.

If the camp day in the early years began with a parody, it is perhaps appropriate that this note on camp songs should end with another from 1907 that the leaders sang to the children every night as they went to their rooms to bed down to the tune of "Auld Lang Syne":

"Sleep sweet, within thy quiet rooms,
My friends, where'er thou art,
And let no mournful yesterdays
Disturb thy peaceful heart.

Nor let tomorrow scare thy rest
With dreams of coming ill,
For God is watching overhead,
His care surrounds thee still.

Forget thyself and all the world,
Put out each feverish light
The stars are shining overhead
Sleep sweet, goodnight, goodnight.
(The stars are shining overhead,
Sleep sweet, goodnight, goodnight . . .)

POSTSCRIPT

It is also proper to bring *The Camp Wise Story* to a close with a song, "Goodby Camp Wise," a parody of a popular tune "Goodbye Girls, I'm Through," from the 1914 Broadway musical "Chin-Chin" by Ivan Caryll and John Golden, which the campers sang as they left with the hope of coming back another year:

> *Goodbye camp, we're through,*
> > *We say farewell to you,*
> *The hours are so few*
> > *'Till we must say a'doo;*
> *We're through with our vacation,*
> > *But we have an invitation*
> *To come back each coming year,*
> > *Goodbye camp, goodbye camp,*
> *Goodbye Camp Wise, to you.*

Index

COLOPHON

This book was composed by Professional Book Compositors, Inc., Lorain, Ohio, typeset in Goudy Oldstyle and printed on Arbor paper. It was printed and perfect bound by Edwards Brothers, Inc., Ann Arbor, Michigan.

Designed by Mort Epstein of Epstein, Gutzwiller & Partners, Inc., Cleveland, Ohio.